*Essays
Out of
My Life*

On Second Thought

DONALD W. SHRIVER, JR.

Books by Donald W Shriver, Jr.

The Unsilent South: Prophetic Preaching in Racial Crisis (1965)

How Do You Do and Why: Christian Ethics for Young People (1966)

Rich Man Poor Man: Christian Ethics for Modern Man (1972)

Spindles and Spires: A Re-Study of Religion and Social Change in Gastonia, with John Earle and Dean D. Knudsen (1976)

Is There Hope for the City?, with Karl A. Ostrom (1977)

The Gospel, the Church, and Social Change (1980)

Medicine and Religion: Strategies of Care, editor (1980)

Redeeming the City: Theology, Politics, and Urban Policy, with Ronald D. Pasquariello and Alan Geyer (1982)

The Lord's Prayer: A Way of Life (1983)

Altered Landscapes: Christianity in America 1935–85: Essays in Honor of Robert T. Handy, with David W. Lotz and John F. Wilson, editors (1989)

Beyond Success: Corporations and Their Critics in the 1990s, with James Kuhn (1991)

An Ethic for Enemies: Forgiveness in Politics (1995)

Honest Patriots: Loving a Country Enough to Remember Its Misdeeds (2005)

H. Richard Niebuhr (Abingdon Pillars of Theology) (2009)

On Second Thought: Essays Out of My Life (2010)

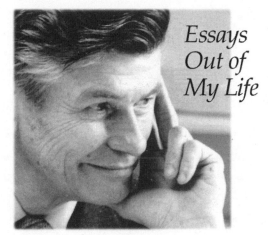

*Essays
Out of
My Life*

On Second
Thought

DONALD W. SHRIVER, JR.

Seabury Books

NEW YORK

Cover art courtesy of John H. Popper
Cover design by Laurie Klein Westhafer
Page design and typesetting by MediaLynx

Library of Congress Cataloging-in-Publication Data

Shriver, Donald W.
On second thought : essays out of my life / Donald W. Shriver, Jr.
   p. cm.
Includes bibliographical references.
ISBN 978-1-59627-109-8 (pbk.)
1. Christian life. 2. Christian literature, American. I. Title.
BV4510.3.S57 2010
277.3'083092—dc22
[B]
             2009047623

Seabury Books
445 Fifth Avenue
New York, New York 10016

www.seaburybooks.com

An imprint of Church Publishing Incorporated

5 4 3 2 1

To Our Great-Grandchildren

and

In Memoriam
Our Son
Gregory Bruce Shriver

CONTENTS

PREFACE

Anyone who has lived eighty-two years and, during forty-five of them, regularly published books, is vulnerable to the thought: "Time to write a memoir?"

I have resisted that thought, along with its kin, "Time for an autobiography?" Neither achievement nor career, in my estimation, deserves so formidable a retrospect from me. Ethically and theologically assessed, every human life probably deserves an autobiography, but—as the author of the Gospel of John suggested—all the books which might well be written would overflow the capacities of humans to store or read. Completing a book has always left me with a feeling of incompletion. There was so much more to say, too little time or space for saying it.

On the other hand, my life has been filled with events and circumstances that have challenged me to write about them from the perspectives of the field of Christian Social Ethics. I have addressed many of the issues in the field from time to time, but most often under the scholarly constraints of so-called objectivity, which require a minimum of personal input from one's life situation. It has often puzzled me that speakers will begin a speech with "apologies for a personal illustration." Too bad: often what we most want to know about speakers and teachers is what sort of personal experience has brought them to this stage or this line of thought.

Often the pages that we scholars write are already indebted to life experiences that go unacknowledged. When, as in a 1976 book on the relation of churches to a local textile community, I dared to introduce some biographical background to the research, one reviewer protested that personal stories have no place in scholarship about society. Since then, my suspicions have grown that personal experience does influence how one thinks and writes. To hide its influence is to be dishonest and opaque.

That 1976 book, *Spindles and Spires*, twelve years in the writing, was a confluence of themes that occupied the first half of my career as a minister and scholar. The book was a sequel to the 1940 study of one of my Yale Professors, Liston Pope, *Millhands and Preachers*. Because of that book's careful study of the role of churches in the social-economic life of Gastonia, North Carolina, I sought and accepted a call to be the minister of a Presbyterian Church in that small city in the late 1950s. Ten years later I was back in Gastonia to research a book on the subject in the company of two young sociologists. My three years as a pastor in that textile community set the agenda of my graduate work at Harvard around the theme: how does religious faith affect—or fail to affect—the ethics of church members in relation to great social issues like race relations, economic justice, and war? In those three years I encountered the difficulty that many Christians seem to have in translating one of the great doctrines of Christianity, the forgiveness of sins, into personal and social meaning. The Gastonia book ended with several pages of observation about how the city of Gastonia needed a social version of forgiveness if it were ever to recover collectively from its traumatic textile strike of 1929, a trauma central to the history recalled in both books. Later, in 1983, I wrote *The Lord's Prayer: A Way of Life*, a study of the implications of that prayer for the social-ethical perspectives of Christians. A key chapter explored the radical two-dimensional teaching of Jesus that divine and human forgiveness are inseparable and interdependent.

My doctoral thesis at Harvard on the theology of forgiveness and the work of social psychiatrists was a systematic exploration of this theme. It matured thirty years later in my 1995 book, *An Ethic for Enemies: Forgiveness in Politics*. In the interval between my thesis and that book, I had studied and participated in the Civil Rights Movement of the 1960s and published, as the first of my fifteen books, *The Unsilent South*, a collection of sermons delivered in southern pulpits during that crisis. The quotation from Robert Walkup in the essay on the church that follows here picks up a thread of social ethics which runs through my life and work: the dire consequences of racism in human life worldwide. The essay "1969" revolves around the crises of racial justice and war in that era in America, especially as those crises impacted my son. My 2005 sequel to *An Ethic for Enemies* was *Honest Patriots*, which centers on the legacies of racism in Germany, South Africa, and the United States. In these books, and in numerous other articles and public speeches, I have tried to express particular amazement and gratitude at the role of African-American churches and leaders in overcoming the split between personal and socially conscious religion. With unique consistency, they have practiced a form of forgiveness in response to the insults to their humanity documented in the racist legacy that still haunts the history of the United States.

Kindred questions of economic justice have occupied me over the years, echoed in the next-to-last essay here, "Money." Here I owe a large debt to my colleague James Kuhn, with whom I taught classes in business ethics at Columbia University in the 1980s. That classroom experience with theology and business school students resulted in our 1991 book on the social responsibility of business corporations, *Beyond Success*. Like four of my other books, this one shared authorship with a colleague from a discipline different from my own. Especially for addressing the complex ethical questions of modern human life, we need the help of more than one expert. I have often quoted Will Rogers, "All of us are ignorant, only in different areas." I like a positive form of that: "All of us are knowledgeable, only in different areas." Long ago Aristotle observed that all humans seem to think that they know something about ethics. In fact, all do. For the study of "social ethics" in particular, we need to listen to many neighbors' voices.

Similarly, it was colleagues at North Carolina State University who first stirred my interests in ecology. In 1969, three of us—a biologist, a historian, and I—developed that university's first interdisciplinary academic course on the subject. Echoes of that experience can be found in the essay here, "When Ecology Becomes Personal: Ten Acres." To my work in that university and church life, I owe much of my devotion to forms of administration that suit the goals of education, an interest that finally flourished in my sixteen years of work as president of a theological seminary, described at length in the essay, "Leadership."

The first essays of this book concern subjects on which I have seldom written before—books, friends, and music. The rest are direct descendants of fifty years of work that wove together the disparate threads of theology, ethics, and history, all in contexts of active challenges that expressed a combination of theory native to my profession with my responsibilities as a citizen. When I first proposed this book to my longtime friend and distinguished editor Davis Perkins, I said: "How about short essays around topics that have intrigued me over the years? Spare of footnotes, allusive to my biography, reflective of the contexts that have shaped my personal experience?" His positive response was liberating: "Yes, write it from the heart."

I have gladly tried to follow his instruction, which gave me the opportunity to express some thoughts that have lain dormant in this or that corner of my mind and memory that—for all their dormancy—are matters worth keeping up front in any life.

The result here will not pass for scholarship in the view of some of my friends. The footnotes and quotations from others are rare. My Yale teacher, H. Richard Niebuhr, apologized in the preface to one of his books for his inability to identify all the outside sources of his intellectual life, so deeply had he absorbed those sources in making them his own. Were I actually to write a memoir, I would have to confess to a similar frustration. Who can be sure that anything he or she thinks is truly original? Were we all required to name all our sources, who could identify or count them all? If I were actually to count the number of people who have influenced me in my eight-two years, I would have to imitate the psalmist's wonder at the stars: "If I would count them, they are more than the sand" (Psalms 139:18). I would always begin the counting with the one person to whom I owe the greatest debt of my life, Peggy Shriver. But standing in the wings of my life stage are a crowd of others, known and unknown donors who have made my life rich. To them all, I am forever grateful.

Donald W. Shriver, Jr.
Winter 2010

Chapter 1

Companions of the Mind: Books

೪

We read to know that we are not alone.

—*C.S. Lewis*

There are today, in the living world, only
two systems capable of unlimited heredity,
that is, of transmitting an indefinitely large
number of different messages: these are
the genetic system and human language.[1]

—*Maynard Smith*

D ata on human debts to things long past abound in the news. Astronomers tell us that every chemical in our bodies originated in that star-forming explosion, the Big Bang, or soon thereafter. Biologists say that our personal DNA links us with our most ancient ancestors from Africa, who lived perhaps fifty-million years ago. We would not be here if—ages ago—algae, green plants, and our lungs had not developed their symbiotic exchanges of oxygen and carbon dioxide. "The human person is composed of stardust, fossil stardust."[2]

No human will ever total all the mysteries of our emergence from these deep pasts. But these scientific discoveries have showered us with reasons to be grateful, in every moment of our lives, for our cosmic debts. From the beginning, did "it" have us in mind? I am no warrior in the current battle over "intelligent design," but as a believer in the Creator I have to welcome the language of astrophysicist Marek Demianski: "Somebody had to tune it very precisely." Similarly, Freeman J. Dyson adds: "...it almost seems as if the universe must in some sense have known that we were coming."[3]

As for a daily, more immediate reminder of our human debts to the past, however, nothing quite compares to the ink-tracks on this printed page. By inventing language and then writing, as Loren Eiseley said, our forbears communicate with us through the doors of their tombs. Like us, they believed that they were entrusted with messages which had to be passed on to another generation.[4] There is something wonderful and awesome about these words that our ancestors spoke and passed on to us. Though dead, they yet speak.[5] They speak in words that we daily use. They invented these meaningful sounds. They gave it all to us to use as our minds and tongues find fitting.

It is natural for anyone who has luxuriated in a career in education to ponder these verbal debts. The two apartments in which all my New York years have been spent are each a hundred years old. I often say a silent "thank you" to the hands of the carpenters, the stone masons, the painters, and the architects who built these rooms. They are all dead, but their hands are here in the walls. I do not have to wait until Labor Day to be thankful for them. Furniture makers still live in the chairs in which I daily sit. They have furnished much comfort for my sitting and sleeping. In a like manner, on the walls sit the furniture of my *mind*: several thousand books intimately related to my intellectual and spiritual biography. When I stare up at those shelves and ponder the time scale of their origins, I implicitly acknowledge about 5,000 years of human effort to speak to unknowable descendants like myself. By loving books, I also acknowledge the gifts of ancient manuscript copiers and printing presses. If money is congealed work, books are congealed mind. They testify to what my neighbors of the past have thought, done, and yearned for.

There is a somber side to the sheer existence of some of those shelved books. Some would not be there without the determination of the authors to resist forces bent on making sure that I would never get to read them. I think of a man named Baruch, who was secretary to the Hebrew prophet Jeremiah. When the king of Judah found Jeremiah's writing a threat to kingly power and prestige, he had the papyri burned, leaf by leaf. At that, the prophet and Baruch wrote it all down again, plus "many similar words" (Jeremiah 36:32). How this repeat-version survived the subsequent imprisonment of Jeremiah and his exile to Egypt, we do not know. But anonymous others did preserve the second edition; otherwise, we would not have the Book of Jeremiah. We owe the survival of the book to determined political resisters.

Political powers who burn books set a precedent for burning people. Across the street from the former University of Berlin, there now rests in the pavement a transparent square of glass covering a below ground arrangement of white, empty book shelves. This is the spot where, on May 10, 1933, Hitler's police supervised the burning of hundreds of books from that university's libraries deemed unfit for the eyes of good Germans. Students and faculty joined in the bonfire. Around the perimeter of that little square is now engraved a line from the nineteenth century German poet, Heinrich Heine: "Wherever they burn books they will also, in the end, burn human beings." So it would be in Nazi Germany.

Science and common wisdom teach us that, without the companionship of other living beings, none of us would live physically for long. For the mind and spirit, many of us would not live for long without books. Consider Robert Sobukwe, leader of the Pan-African Congress in the 1950s, and eloquent opponent of South Africa's apartheid regime. He was so eloquent, in fact, that the white parliament voted annually to continue confining him to a little cottage on Robben Island and to deny him material for reading and all conversation with other humans. Sobukwe finally went mad. We know from American prison records that, continued for years, solitary confinement leads to insanity. Some would call it "nonviolent" punishment. In fact, it is torture. To be sure, in these days of electric media, not every literate person has my high regard for books. A young computer-savvy friend once walked into our apartment and, looking up at that wall covered with books, exclaimed, "Soon we will have no need of books." To say that to a scholar of my age is like saying: "Electronics will eliminate the food you have been eating all these years. We have other means of nourishment. Learn to use them."

Of course, electronics can also transform the books on my shelves into digital books. These electronic books have many advantages. Travelers can take with them dozens of books in that little pocket-sized box. The hard-of-seeing can magnify the print. Moreover, as long as one copy of any book still exists on earth, it can be recovered for millions of new readers as is seldom possible for books dubbed "out of print." Not yet possessing an electronic book, I shall probably buy one. I think I will first test it by seeing if it will permit me to buy a copy of my 1965 book, *The Unsilent South*.

My guess is that Marshall McLuhan was close to the historic dynamics of a human thirst for communication when he noted that technologies pileup on each other. They complement more than destroy. Telephone lines morph into the internet, film cameras into digitals, slow mail into email, newspapers into websites. But none of these inventions dispense with the more ancient arts of spoken and written language. Nor do any of our new gadgets have our permission to ignore the biological gifts and limitations of human eyes, ears, and hands. An electronic device for reading a book online while we ride the bus must still fit our hands and suit our eyes. Conceivably, by installing computerized systems in our brains, we might someday have behind our eyes, so to speak, all the information stored in our brains that before we secured from books. We might come to resemble the Borg in *Star Trek*. But mere information is not history, narrative, and wisdom. Furthermore, pursuing one's own interests across an infinite number of websites is not the same as a long adventure of thought that lies in our hands when we first open some author's book. We may discover that it is intellectual trash or that it is treasure. Read, digested, and cherished, the latter are our nominations for great books.

As objects on our shelves, they can become icons. Like the lares and penates of old Roman households, they may take up only a little corner space. But they remind the household of its ultimate concerns. They sit in that space surrounded by a glow from the minds of their readers. To pick up one such book is often to pause as it rests in one's hand, a pause of respect, gratitude, and love.

Linear thought is not the only service that books render to one's mind, but they are solid protections against the illusion, fostered by news bits and sound bites, that the condensed version of any communication will suffice "for all practical purposes." A certain professor assigned Shakespeare's *Romeo and Juliet* to her English class, and one student shrugged, "Don't need to read it. I already know the story." This response deserves a reply that distinguishes truth from information. Shakespeare-on-the-page and Shakespeare-on-the-stage mean to become Shakespeare-in-the-mind of an audience. Via poetry and drama, the playwright invites new generations to join the agony and ecstasy of human loves and hates. Like any good play, a great book draws the reader into a performance. At age eighteen and a recent draftee, in a summer off-duty evening in Fort Jackson, South Carolina, I visited the post library and picked off the shelf *The Dialogues of Plato.* Turning to "The Apology of Socrates," I looked in vain to discover what Socrates had to "apologize" for. Instead, I learned a new use of the word and joined one of those critical dialogues of human history: is there any cause, any truth, worth dying for? On that evening in a military library, with sun streaming through the windows, a man about to be wrongly executed by his city state touched my spirit as he had already touched millions of others worldwide. It was my first real introduction to the intellectual and spiritual world of the Greeks.

I can now celebrate dozens of such encounters with my human predecessors in the books that they left behind. My feelings about them linger. Psychologists know that feelings can persist long after one forgets their particulars. (Why do I remember the beams of sun streaming through the windows of that library? It has something to do with the warmth of inner illumination.)

The iconic quality of some books deserves attention. There are a number of well-thumbed books on my shelf that can easily be replaced with newer durable editions. But I will never throw those frayed pages into the fire. Someone else will have to do it. Those books ignited spiritual-mental flames in me. On occasion I reach up and touch worn volumes of Dickens, Tolstoy, Eiseley, Polanyi, Bernanos, Buber, Wiesel—not to speak of several yards of my favorite theologians. I cherish these volumes with whiffs of recollection of the summer months when I first read some of them. I have forgotten some characters in Dickens' *Bleak House* and Tolstoy's *War and Peace*, but I re-experience some of the feelings they left in me every time I pause to note those books on my shelves.

As for the theologians: I have a special set of feelings for one ragged paperback, now fifty years old. It was printed on paper familiar to anyone who remembers the poor quality of paper used during World War II and immediately thereafter. In fact the paper on which these pages were originally written was poorer quality yet: newsprint and toilet paper, some of it. The book is *Letters and Papers from Prison* by Dietrich Bonhoeffer. Like many readers of his works worldwide, it was my doorway to the mind and spirit of one of the great Christians of the twentieth century. The book consists mostly of letters which he wrote to his friend Eberhard Bethge, then in the German army in Italy. Both participated in the July 20, 1944, plot to assassinate Adolf Hitler. For that, Bonhoeffer paid with his life; Bethge almost did so.

Obviously we cherish the physical form of some books because we have learned to cherish their contents. Of no book is that more likely than the ones which some community of readers has named "sacred scripture." Nobody among faithful Jews, Christians, and Muslims likes to see their sacred texts thrown into the trash can. Most have rules for careful burning of the old frayed things. For believers and their life-world, these books are no ordinary things.

A yard of Bible translations occupy my shelves, along with many yards of books written about that Bible. Without an acquaintance with the Bible, Bonhoeffer would not have written his letters as he did, nor ordered his life in some deep conformity with the book's message. I will not pause here to justify the belief that in this book a careful reader can hear the Word of God in words that "will not pass away." I have always admired the answer of the evangelist D.L. Moody to the question, "Why do you know that the Bible is inspired?" His simple reply: "Because it inspires me." Were I to converse with such a questioner at length, I would want to amplify that testimony. Skeptics might be surprised at a primary theme of my amplifying: "Because it is the most human and humanizing book I have ever read."

Another story from political prisoners in the 1940s sticks in my memory. A cellmate asked his companion why he read the Bible so much when there were other books at hand. The answer: "Because it doesn't tell lies about human beings." In a very straightforward sense, the Bible narrates true stories of humans-good and humans-bad in a mixture that makes it easy for any reader to sense kinship with these characters of old. Whether flavored with myth or credible historical fact, the stories are populated with real, believable people. On the myth side, the first three chapters of Genesis were surely conceived as dramatic portrayals of our human experience of each other and ourselves. Genesis 1–3 echoes something vital and beautiful, tragic and painful, in gifts once ours and now lost in our histories with each other. The Genesis story is "timeless" in the sense that it goes on all the time. We overreach our limitations, yet we resent them while knowing that we must observe them. We yield to the overreach and become partners in crime—Adam and Eve's. Then we blame each other in the chatter that infects human conversation when we are afraid of truth. Why all our concern for the naked human body? Somehow we have been persuaded not to uncover too much of ourselves. . . . So go the "somehow" myths of Genesis, telling truth about ourselves in poetic drama.

In the later, more historical Hebrew and Christian biblical narratives, the actors are also a mixed lot. All of them, much like us: conversing from time to time in stammering ways with the Creator, stumbling into what it means to experience the presence of the Almighty, stumbling into repetitions of the folly of an Adam and Eve. Abraham tells a lie to protect himself against a wily Egyptian ruler; Isaac plays favorites with his sons; one of Isaac's sons tells lies galore to his future father-in-law; and in a blatant mixture of jealousy and prestige-hunger, that family—the twelve sons of Jacob—lays groundwork for their descendants' descent into civil war. In this story, every home on earth gets alerted to the danger of idolizing "family values."

Echoes of this realism suffuse the Hebrew Bible, and nowhere louder than in the domestic-political relations of the greatest of their kings—David. He lusts after a beautiful woman, makes her pregnant, then has her husband murdered. So it goes: the Bible busily keeps its readers safe from idealizing humans, even the best of us, keeping true to the faith that the Creator of this planet and all the stars is active in it all to bring something good to pass. Do not despair of this mixture of good and evil; there is promise in this thing. There is treasure in this cracked human vessel. You, your ancestors, and your descendants are objects of a love more powerful than you can imagine.

Of course the Bible does imagine it. We read the book

and catch glimpses of what it imagines, a glimpse encased in such human pain as Hosea's in relation to his adulterous wife, a Roman government's greatest-ever mistake in executing Jesus of Nazareth, and the guilty misery of disciples who stood by letting it happen without saying a word. It does take considerable faith to consider this book, full of such people, as the Word of God. If there is light here, it comes to us by penetrating our own shadows.

People of faith who read the Bible in faith are companions of D. L. Moody. More profoundly—so goes the orthodox view of biblical inspiration—they are companions of the Spirit of the One who cares for us up close. This Bible, says the doctrine, becomes the Word of God only insofar as the Spirit "guides you into all the truth" (John 16:13). This is the real promise in Bible-reading. It makes this book very special indeed.

But it is special, too, in its permission to us to find links between its texts and other texts. Fresh from a deep reading of Jeremiah and the Gospel of John, one might risk being called a heretic for suggesting that something like the Holy Spirit hovers over readers of Augustine's *Confessions*, Shakespeare's *King Lear*, Dostoevsky's *Brothers Karamazov*, Wiesel's *Night*, and the autobiography of Nelson Mandela. Something like the Spirit of the Evil One hovers over some other books—Hitler's *Mein Kampf* comes to mind. Such books should provoke us to "test the spirits to see whether they are of God" (I John 4:1). The Bible itself contains the primary tests. But there are other, complementary tests, as Karl Barth suggested when he remarked that "Christians should sleep over neither their Bibles nor their newspapers." To stand looking down at those dusty white shelves memorializing the burning of books on 10 May, 1933, in Berlin is to know our need for all possible help for protection against evil spirits. Almost alone among vocal church leaders, a few days after Hitler's ascent to power,

Bonhoeffer publicly identified the anti-Semitism in Nazism. Had he never read the newspapers and a lot of history, as well as the Bible, he could hardly have recognized so promptly this evil at work in the core of Nazism. Real reverence for the Bible calls for some parallel reading. And to that, the experience of Christians adds: it calls for some living human companions, too. It calls the lonely reader to seek consulting interpreters. Sometimes they are fellow readers in a church. Sometimes, like Jeremiah and Bonhoeffer, they speak from jails.

Perhaps of all the protections that the Bible and the Spirit furnish the readers of books, none is more important than protection against idolization of books themselves, including this scripture and every other. One is not a believer in the Bible if one has not discovered how it points away from itself to the One with whom we all "have to do"—the Author of all things, our Creator, the One to whom Jesus prayed. Biblical literalists do not like having this called to their attention: that well-thumbed book, which to read is often to be inspired, is not in itself divine. Indeed, the One to whom it points seems intent on pointing away from even the divine self to all those creations that She loves and bids us love—ailing earth species and our ailing human neighbors. "As you did it to one of the least of these . . . you did it to me" (Matthew 25:40).

People like me like nothing better than sinking into the reverie prompted by the reading of a great book. But some of the greatness of the Bible consists in its regular message to its readers: Get up; you have other work to do.

I love books. But great books call me to love my neighbors.

NOTES

1 Maynard Smith quoted in Holmes Rolston III, *Three Big Bangs:Matter-Energy, Life, Mind* (New York: Columbia University Press, forthcoming 2010), chapter 2.

2 Holmes Rolston III, *Science and Religion: A Critical Survey* (New York: Random House, 1987), 67.

3 Ibid., 69.

4 Loren Eiseley, *The Unexpected Universe* (New York: Harcourt, Brace and World, 1969), 117.

5 See Hebrews 11:4.

Chapter 2

More Gift than Achievement: Friends

Think where man's glory most begins and ends,
And say my glory was I had such friends.
—*W.B. Yeats*
The Municipal Gallery Revisited

I count myself in nothing so happy
As in a soul remembering my good friends
—*William Shakespeare*, Richard II,
Act 2, Scene 3, line 46.

Not to have any is not really to be human. To lose them to death is the beginning of one's own.

My father, before his death at age ninety-six, said frequently, "Almost all of my friends are gone." Without them, he implied, becoming old was no blessing. Many of his friends were fellow members of his local Methodist congregation. At his funeral in 1997, it was a shock to realize how small a cluster of folk gathered to celebrate his life. His round of living friends had shrunk drastically. The rich human network of his life in Norfolk, Virginia, could not be imagined from that ceremony.

The late novelist Kurt Vonnegut once remarked on the peculiar mixture of folk in one's extended family. You return home for the sad occasion of a funeral and are reminded that you do not deeply *like* everyone among your gathered relatives. Well, said Vonnegut, "families are not there to be liked. They are just there—to be family." Some may be friends, some not.

Friends are gifts arriving in one's life without notice or asking. Childhood and grammar school would have been very difficult for me without the help and companionship of friends near my age. The trauma of my first day in first grade sticks in my memory as the day I got lost in the school basement. Maury Yates, a boy who knew me from our neighborhood, rescued me, tears and all. He remains locked in my memory as a person who befriended me in a distress common to any child's first adventures into public spaces. Wordsworth knew about this in his tribute to "little, nameless, unremembered acts of kindness and of love." But in fact we do remember them.

After decades of living in a big American city, no one is likely to disparage such acts of care, no matter how "little" and momentary. In its network of impersonal relationships, city life haunts us all with the suspicion that nobody in the crowd will give more than passing attention to us if we fall down, break a leg, get run over, or have a heart attack. My experience as a thirty-year New Yorker contradicts this fear. Somebody in the crowd invariably springs to your aid. Somebody calls the police or an ambulance. New Yorkers are famous for minding their own business, but deep down they know that neither personal nor collective urban survival is possible without some form of friendship-in-distress. Lawyers, doctors, police, and other caregivers come to our rescue, too. Spontaneous help from strangers keeps urban life human.

That was the lesson that young Vartan Gregorian learned in his first few weeks in urban America, traveling from his native Tabriz, in modern Iran, to become a college student in San Francisco. After a few interim days in New York City, he "wrote home that in New York I felt like an anonymous ant. If they stepped on me they would not even notice me." About to board the plane from New York to San Francisco, he discovered to his horror that he had lost the ticket. Desperate and in tears, he told the ticket agent that he *had* to get to San Francisco. To his relief, the agent replied, "You can board the plane. But you must stay on board all the way." The incident changed his image of New Yorkers. "Even in New York, this massive metropolis, individuals mattered. After all, I was not an insignificant, anonymous ant."[1]

His experience reminded me of the time when, at the same age, I found myself marooned in Cincinnati without funds enough to buy a train ticket for home. By phone my father advised me: "Tell the conductor that I will pay him when you arrive in Norfolk." When I did so, that conductor said to me: "Your name is Shriver. I knew your grandfather. He was a Pullman conductor on this line. I know that we can trust your father and you."

I would not advise any modern urban traveler to count on personal favors of this ilk in our cash-conscious, ticket-demanding, credit card suffused culture! But without these episodic forms of friendship, we all might find ourselves prisoners of emergencies.

Such friendships pale in comparison, however, with long-lasting human connections we identify as "good friends." Harvard researchers in the 1950s found that tolerable personal survival in cities requires at least three or four people whose help you can count on for the long haul. The most radical version of such friendship is marriage: "in sickness and in health, in joy and in sorrow, in plenty and in want, as long as we both shall live." (That particular friendship deserves the attention given it in chapter 10 of this collection.) When real and enduring, marriage is a very special form of friendship. In a film set in a retirement home and starring Hume Cronym, Cronym's character comments to a nurse about his deceased wife, "She was my best friend, you know."

She was the best in a category we like to call "good." Good friends share a certain unconditional loyalty, rare among humans. For most human relationships there have to be some conditions, but to tag friends as "good" sets them in a special group of folk outside of the usual reciprocities of commerce, work, law, and contract. Good friends set a minimum of conditions. Theirs, as a sociologist might say, is an "ascriptive" relation, not "achieved."

Occasionally, we mentally run through our network of friendships when we have to decide if any among them would be willing to assist us in very inconvenient conditions. Several years ago our car broke down on a highway sixty miles north of home. It was a Sunday night, and no taxi or bus answered our calls from a gas station. Would any one of our friends with cars be willing to come get us? We didn't come up with more than two or three nominations. Our first choice was one in New Jersey. He spent two hours and much energy coming to our rescue. To call him, we had mentally to draw lines between acquaintances, colleagues, casual friends, and good ones.

Good friends are more gift than achievement. Over a lifetime they are likely to be few in number, not often more than a dozen or so. They are discernable in memory as those to whom we write longer notes at Christmas and spontaneous "how are you doing?" letters. They are on the top of the list of those we invite to a party, hope to see in travel, call at once when we hear they are sick. As likely as not, we are not fully conscious of how much their existence means to us until the moment we receive news of their deaths. Such was a friend and colleague of mine at North Carolina State University. The last time we saw each other we said: "Let's find time on our next visit to bring each other up to date."But that *next* never came. Ten years of work together in church and academic settings produced a long list of questions we could have pursued together long into retirement.

In the winter of 1947, in the Signal Corps School in Fort Monmouth, New Jersey, I met a fellow draftee from South Carolina. In one conversation we discovered so many common interests that after the army we carried on an extensive, searching correspondence during our four years in different colleges. In 1953, for reasons that needed other friends to make clear to me, he committed suicide. Ever after, I have remembered him as a companion on a journey towards W.H. Auden's "great city that has expected your return for years." At his funeral others testified that he was a young man of remarkable intelligence with an equally remarkable capacity for friendship.

Of all the barriers that inhibit this depth of friendship, none, perhaps, is as high as social or institutional hierarchy. Good friends share and celebrate each other's gifts. They rejoice in differences of talent, knowledge, and experience. But that is hardly to be expected with the people who are superior to us in age, social rank, prestige, or authority. This is the case in all institutions, including the one in which I have spent most of my professional life: higher education. Barriers always stand between students and teachers. After three years as minister of a congregation in North Carolina, I began work at Harvard. In the first month, my adviser cautioned, "You may find it difficult to go from a position in which you had some prestige and authority to being a student again." He was right, but at the end of those three years I shared with some of my fellow graduate students the priceless experience of beginning twenty years of correspondence and other contacts with Professor James Luther Adams, who had an uncanny capacity for turning the relation between professor and student into friendship. As all teachers and students know, it is presumptuous to expect this transition. In the 1960s many students started calling their teachers by first names, not always to the benefit of the teaching-learning relationship. Hierarchies have their purpose. Friendship can emerge in spite of them, but only as a gracious gift.

Occasionally a friendship comes to memory that has not been "tended" for a long time. In my retirement I have begun giving myself the joy of reconnecting with friends who played important parts in my life decades ago. The letter I write to them begins: "It may surprise you, but I have often thought of you at moments when. . . ." In February 1984, it occurred to me that just fifty years previous I had entered third grade. My teacher, Miss Frances Hanbury, was one of my favorites. She was now in her eighties. To her undoubted surprise, I wrote her a letter expressing my conviction that we veterans of graduate school teaching owe more to elementary school teachers than they ever get public credit for. I am sure that when some of my young neighbors in Harlem decide to quit school at age sixteen, they often do so out of painful associations with education. We who teach in graduate schools are beneficiaries of good teachers in elementary and secondary schools. Ours is the luxury of teaching their successes. The failures never reach us.

To be sure, it is risky to wait fifty years to express gratitude to anyone in our past. Belated letters are hostages to mortality. Not long ago I tried reconnecting with a certain college friend only to discover that he had died two years ago. I was accumulating questions that began with, "Have you changed your mind on . . . ?" It was a friendship tended too little, too late.

The Philosophers and Theologians on Friendship

Among the teachers we remember with most affection are those who befriended our *minds*. In my junior year of high school, I complained a bit to my Latin teacher about the boredom of a whole semester of Cicero's *Orations Against Cataline*. She asked me if I would like to substitute that Roman's post-political essay, "De Amicitia." I took to the idea eagerly. I can still remember the line, "He who takes friendship out of life takes away the sunshine."

But brighter light on the subject of friendship comes to me in the Bible. The Bible is a "warts and all" account of human life. Its stress is not on rules for human behavior and (even) on ideas of God, but rather on history in which rules and glimpses of God come alive in concrete human events. The Bible speaks of friends occasionally in exalted terms. Moses talks to God "face to face as a man speaks to his friend"(Exodus 33:11). At the end of the most famous friendship in the biblical history, David laments the death of Saul's son Jonathan, calling him a "brother" whose "love to me was wonderful passing the love of women" (2 Samuel 1:26). (The comparison betrays David's rather defective relationships with women.)

On the whole, the Hebrew Bible portrays human families and friendships as shot through with fallibility. The David history is one long illustration of how loyalties of blood relatives and political friends vary like the weather. *Proverbs* sighs with ambivalence in the matter.

> There are friends who pretend to be friends,
> but there is a friend who sticks closer than
> a brother.
>
> *(Proverbs 18:24)*

> Wealth brings many friends,
> but the poor are left friendless . . .
> If the poor are hated even by their kin,
> how much more are they shunned by
> their friends!
>
> *(Proverbs 19:4,7, NRSV)*

As for friendship in emergencies, Jeremiah and Micah are pessimistic. In wartime, they observed, social trust deteriorates. Neighbor, friend, wife, family member—none is to be trusted.

> Put no trust in a neighbor,
> have no confidence in a friend;
> Guard the doors of your mouth
> [even!] from her who lies in your bosom. . . .
>
> *(Micah 7:5)*

Such shattering of trust, across a full spectrum of human relationships, becomes fact in modern totalitarian societies, as in East Germany under Stasi surveillance. There, wives, husbands, children, colleagues, and friends spied on each other in the service of national security.

In post-9/11 America, we know something about a government that expects such spying on and by all of us: "If you see something, say something," admonishes the subway ad. In the year 2007, some 1,944 New Yorkers did report that they "saw something." But not all of us trusted government itself enough to make such a report. That 1,944—out of a population of eight million—is not very many. Fact is, in 2007 many Americans were not sure of our own government's friendship. In terrorist-conscious America, every citizen can be wire tapped. Amos may have had it right: "He who is prudent will keep silent in such a time; for it is an evil time" (Amos 5:13).

Jeremiah, loneliest prophet of all, had one friend, Baruch, who stood by him in spite of kings, police, prisons, and accusations of treason. To Baruch we apparently owe the survival of a twice-copied written record of the prophet's life and message. Some churches practice the liturgical habit of congregational response to Bible reading, "Thanks be to God!" For our access to the writings of Jeremiah, we ought also to respond, "Thanks be to Baruch!"

With the exception of Moses, the Hebrew Bible seldom speaks of friendship between God and humans. But the possibility of divine-human friendship comes to remarkable expression in Jesus' dealings with his disciples. They once perceived Jesus as briefly enjoying conversational intimacy with God in company with Moses and Elijah (Luke 9:28–36). In less exalted connections, Jesus often addresses another person as "friend." His parables are full of casual mention of friends, some "good," some fair-weather. In his typical "how much more" way of comparing human and divine-human relationships, he imagines a friend's need for food to serve a midnight guest (Luke 11:5–80). He knocks on another friend's door at that hour. The knock is unwelcome, rousing a family from sleep. Jesus says that the sleepy friend will finally push some bread out of the window by dint of the urgency of the request. In his *a fortiori* analogy from things human to things divine, he asks: If that happens among finite friends, what might happen from a knock on the door of the Infinite?

> "If you then, who are evil, know how to give good gifts to your children [and importuning friends] how much more will the heavenly Father give the Holy Spirit to those who ask him" (Luke 11:13)?

One word for that Spirit in the New Testament is *Parakletos*, one "called to the side of" another. This is an image richly associated with the practical help of good friends. In his final conversation with his disciples before his death, Jesus assures them that they are his friends, not his servants. He is about to "lay down his life for his friends" (John 14:16, 14:25, 15:26, 16:7, 16:13). Even in this final conversation of Jesus with his disciples, however, the context is down-to-earth human finitude: dying on behalf of one's friends in the real time of one's real life. It is an intimidating test of friendship. The disciples are not yet up to it: "All the disciples forsook him and fled" (Matthew 26:36). Broken, conditional, finite friends that we all are, we understand that flight. The biblical narrative leaves many of us with the question: Would I really be willing to lay down my life for a friend?

The Communion of Saintly Friends

No theological saint in my life has posed this very question more personally than Dietrich Bonhoeffer. Many American theologians of my generation admired, read, and remembered his example of friendship with Eberhard Bethge. Again and again, admirers of Bonhoeffer recall the image of his decision in July 1939 to return to Nazi Germany from the safety of New York. In his parting note to Reinhold Niebuhr, he explained his conviction that "I will have no right to participate in the reconstruction of Christian life in Germany after the war if I do not share the trials of this time with my people. . . ." He did not expect to be a martyr, but clearly he knew the risks.[2]

Bonhoeffer would probably not have called his decision to return to Germany an act of friendship, but he certainly felt it to be a directive of the Spirit that he should join the Resistance against Hitler for putting a "spoke in the wheel" of the Nazi machine, whatever the risk to his own life. He always insisted that a Christian must "do the truth" and not rest content with just knowing the truth. That is the intimidating feature of his legacy. How much sacrifice ought anyone consider making on behalf of human neighbors suffering from the evildoing of a government? Whose enmity should I risk on behalf of friendship with people put at risk by actions of my own government? Those prisoners in Guantanamo? All those Iraqis still dying in an eight-year-old war? Dark-skinned people stopped arbitrarily by local police? Mexicans risking their lives to cross our borders?

Whatever our answers to those disturbing questions, we ought to remember that we owe our access to Bonhoeffer's writings to his best friend, Eberhard Bethge, who shared similar risks in his connection to the Resistance Movement in wartime Germany. Bethge was Bonhoeffer's Baruch. He made it his vocation for the next fifty-five years to discover, verify, preserve, edit, and tell the life story of his friend in one of the century's great biographies. As Bethge said late in his life, after Bonhoeffer's death "our friendship continued in a transformed way," involving, "so to speak, the whole world in this continuation of our relationship of loyalty."[3]

Many in my generation remember when we first picked up the little book which introduced us to Bonhoeffer, *Letters and Papers from Prison*. My 1963 copy had come from England, printed on low-quality wartime paper easily reducible to confetti. I have in my home study a 1991 photo of Eberhard Bethge holding in his hand the original of his favorite letter, that of July 21, 1944, the day after the failure of the plot to assassinate Hitler. On that day Bonhoeffer knew that his death would ensue. It did the following April. The letter contains a paragraph that would become one of the most famous bits of theology of the next sixty years.

> I'm still discovering, right up to this moment,
> that it is only by living completely in this
> world that one learns to have faith. . . .
> This is what I mean by this-worldliness.
> I mean living unreservedly in life's duties,
> problems, successes and failures, experiences
> and perplexities. In so doing we throw
> ourselves completely into the arms of God,
> taking seriously, not our own sufferings,
> but those of God in the world—watching
> with Christ in Gethsemane. That, I think,
> is faith; that is *metanoia*; and that is how
> one becomes a man and a Christian. (See
> Jeremiah 45).[4]

In Jeremiah 45, referred to in Bonhoeffer's letter, the Lord speaks to Baruch, "Do you seek great things for yourself? Seek them not." Leave to God the rest of human history.

Eberhard Bethge died at age ninety-one in the year 2000. Six years earlier, in a lecture given in English in Boston, he finally was persuaded to fill out the background of his dozen years of knowing his friend in "Bonhoeffer's Theology of Friendship." In it, he quotes a letter written to him on Dietrich's thirty-fifth birthday in 1941, two years before the Gestapo took him to prison.

> . . . [T]he human heart is created in such
> a way that it seeks and finds refuge in the
> singular rather than in the plural. . . . There

are individual relationships without loyalty
and loyalty without individual relationships.
Both are to be found in the plural. But
together (which is seldom enough!) they
seek the singular, and happy is he who
"succeeds in this great luck."[5]

Bethge quotes from Schiller's "Ode to Joy" as appropriated in Beethoven's Ninth Symphony. He comments that this description of friendship is empirical, not overtly rooted in theological concepts. "It flows out of an act of accepting a gift and not from the arduousness of dogmatic logical deductions. . . ." It comes to two persons as acts of freedom, "open to fruitful illogic." Later from prison, on January 23, 1944, Bonhoeffer celebrated that freedom: "I believe that within the sphere of this freedom friendship is by far the rarest and most priceless treasure." It belongs to the world of work, government, and family only "as the cornflower belongs to the corn field." No one expects it to bloom there. No one worked to put it there. It just emerged, as the most beautiful spot in the field.[6] The image persists in DB's post–July 21 poem, "The Friend," sent as part of his last surviving letter to Bethge who was then in Italy. For the next eight months Bonhoeffer would be incommunicado, shuffled from prison to prison. The poem expands images of friendship beyond that of the "useless," priceless beauty of the cornflower to the high use of one faithful companion to another.

> Like a clear fresh lake
> in which the spirit cleans off the dust of the day,
> in which it cools itself from the burning heat
> and steels itself in the hour of fatigue—
> like a fortress, to which, from danger and
>   confusion,
> the spirit returns,
> in which it finds refuge, comfort, and strength,
> is a friend to a friend.[7]

This final word passing between two friends was "worldly" in the best Bonhoefferian sense. Neither had to remind the other of Psalm 46. Yes, "*God* is our refuge and strength, a very present help in trouble." But that faith was embedded now in a particular friendship, which needed no theological tag for underscoring its reality. God was "very present" in this deep trouble, anonymously, in the concretion of a gift that was soon to end in death, "in order, just because of that end, to resume a transformed life later on."

The new life began to reach an international public in the first translations of *Letters and Papers* in 1952. It would be followed by many thousands of pages of Bonhoeffer's primary written works and a profusion of secondary studies in many languages. Ten years later that crumbly copy of the *Letters* fell into my hands. It would be the beginning of my membership in an expanding fellowship of others who found in Bonhoeffer a new way of living in the presence of God—solidly in the world, in the suffering of one's neighbors. Among many spiritual friends of Bonhoeffer would be a few who would be my analogy to the Dietrich-Eberhard friendship, beginning with David and Sunyong Suh in Korea, and Helmut and Erika Reihlen in Berlin.

My life has not much imitated the depth and breadth of Bonhoeffer's costly witness to God's truth, justice, and mercy. But now, when I read and remember all that Bethge enabled us to remember of that witness, all that our other friends embody of this fellowship, I am no longer intimidated by either Jesus or Bonhoeffer! None of us lacks concrete presences of God in our day's life; none of us lacks gifts of loyalty that embody the Spirit's invitation to reciprocal loyalties and still-possible sacrifices of love. The possibility of counting myself a member of the Communion of Saints is fulfilled in the present fact and strength of these my worldly friendships. Who would not thank God for them?

NOTES

1 Vartan Gregorian, *The Road Home: My Life and Times* (New York: Simon and Schuster, 2003), 97–98.

2 See Eberhard Bethge, *Dietrich Bonhoeffer* (New York: Harper and Row, 1970), 559.

3 This and several following quotations are from Bethge's essay, "Dietrich Bonhoeffer's Theology of Friendship," *Friendship and Resistance: Essays on Dietrich Bonhoeffer* (Grand Rapids: Eerdmans, 1995), 80–104.

4 Dietrich Bonhoeffer, *Letters and Papers from Prison* (Enlarged Touchstone Edition; ed. Eberhard Bethge. New York: Simon and Schuster, 1997), 369–70.

5 Bethge, 88.

6 Ibid., 88, 97.

7 Ibid., 100–101.

8 Ibid., 102.

Chapter 3

Sound from Silence: Beethoven[1]

~~

If I should ever die, God forbid, let this be
my epitaph: *The only proof he needed for the
existence of God was music.*

> —*the late Kurt Vonnegut,*[2]
> A Man Without a Country

Music is a noble gift of God, next to theology.
I would not change my little knowledge of
music for a great deal.

> —*Martin Luther*

D ecember 2007 was the 200th anniversary of Beethoven's completion of his *Fifth Symphony*. For millions since, that work has been a gateway into classical music. I am one of them.

Beethoven was himself a gateway into the Romantic Era of European history. In more than one sense, he was a musical democrat. Symbolic of that was the crowd of Viennese who attended his funeral in March 1827. John N. Burk compares the event with the burial of Mozart in the same city thirty-six years before when the thirty-five-year-old musical genius had been thrown into a pauper's grave. No one had stayed as a witness. Now, 20,000 people walked to the cemetery to honor Beethoven. Most of them, Burk speculates, had never heard a note of Beethoven's music. But "now, a great musician could command as much respect as any prince. The world had changed, and Beethoven had done much to change it, not by what he had exacted, but by a strange power in his music which lifted [human beings] in spite of themselves."[3] A hundred years later, one of those human beings would be myself. In a lecture in Berlin in the spring of 1999, I said to a German audience: "As an adolescent American of the 1940s, I grew up between Hitler and Beethoven."

Strange, that an artist in the history of an enemy nation should become a symbol of the cause for which a war was being fought against that nation. As everyone knows, the famous four notes that began his Fifth Symphony, by coincidence the letter "V" in Morse Code, became a worldwide call of hope for victory over Nazism.

On Second Thought

In my young American case, an eighth grade music teacher in Norfolk, Virginia, had drawn back the curtain on classical music for me. Beethoven had claimed center stage. In 1941, the Fifth Symphony was the major work in the first orchestral concert I ever attended. Soon after, from my income as a morning newspaper deliverer, I had enough money to buy the 78 rpm version of the Fifth by Toscanini and the NBC Symphony. For the next five years, from constant replaying, I wore that recording to a scratchy frazzle.

Apparently the Fifth has not lost its intergenerational appeal. In the 2007–2008 season, the program notes of the New York Philharmonic introduced the audience to the newest member of the orchestra's trumpet section, Matthew Muckey, age twenty-two. "The first piece I fell in love with," Muckey reported, "was Beethoven's Fifth Symphony. I listened to it over and over." On New Year's Day 2007, in WQXR's annual broadcast of the fifty most popular classics as determined by a pole of its listeners, the announcer noted that Beethoven won the largest number of nominations. The Ninth ranked first, the Fifth second. In 2008, the Ninth again was first; second, the Seventh; third, the Fifth.

It is presumptuous, perhaps, for us musical amateurs to think that we have anything meaningful to say about the miracles of music. Theologians like me should not speak casually of "miracles," but I am inclined to think that there is something miraculous about an interlinked chain of phenomena that transmit sounds inside the mind of a deaf genius onto little black lines and spots of a musical manuscript and thence to skilled reproduction in professional performances of that original mental sound, making it accessible to millions of good human ears centuries later.

Music is a spiritual experience. With the late William Sloane Coffin, Jr., many of us overtly religious folk readily confess, "Next to prayer, music has most often comforted me." Some years ago a neighbor in a seat at Avery Fisher Hall spread out her arms and exclaimed, "This is my church!" Her exclamation won't do for me. A concert audience is not a congregation. But I cannot get away from the notion that God's Spirit sometimes speaks to some of us in the deepest moments of music. It is clear from Beethoven's notebooks that he thought so, too.

Raised a Catholic, he seldom frequented the sanctuary of a church, either in the Rhineland of his birth or the Vienna of his career. Arriving in that self-proclaimed musical capital of Europe at age twenty-two, he was already sure that his calling to music was not only that of an extraordinary pianist but equally that of a composer. When at age twenty-five he dared to tag his new F Major sonata "Opus 1," he was already renowned as a fabulous pianist. He dedicated that work to "Mr. Joseph Haydn, Doctor of Music," making no secret of his ambition to join the ranks of Handel, Haydn, and Mozart. At an aristocrat's party one evening, a stranger scoffed at young Ludwig's ambition to be a composer: "My dear young man . . . you are neither a Goethe nor a Handel; and it is not to be expected that you ever will be, for such masters will not be born again." To which the young Beethoven "withdrew in haughty silence."[4]

Beethoven's inner genius came clothed in some very rough garments. In behavior he was a collection of contradictions: preoccupied with vast orderings of sound, but living in rooms cluttered with disorderly sprawl; needing friends but often insulting them; defending commoners in an aristocratic society but yet insulting to his house servants; always in love but never married; prudently respectful of the aristocrats who supported him but claiming to their faces his own aristocracy of *mind*; yearning for public applause but contemptuous of ordinary musical intelligence to the point of "outrageous rudeness." Not a man, in short, whom we mortals of modest endowments would find easy to meet a second time or even a first. Burk says of him: His "taut jaw and lower lip are unable to relax into a smile. He must [rather] break into a guffaw. It was only in music that Beethoven could really smile. Blind anger, frenetic hilarity, depression—he was subject to them all."[5]

One sees something of that mixture in the twisted expression found on Bourdelle's sculptured facial mask of Beethoven in the lobby of Avery Fisher Hall.

His friends, therefore, had to be very forgiving. In awe of his music, they had compassion for him in his fight against his great enemy of thirty years, deafness. When it comes to miracles, for two centuries we concertgoers have wondered how out of deafness could come music. As it closed in upon him, increasingly Beethoven "saw himself shut off from society. There was only music left to him." Somehow, says Burk, "Deafness was not altogether blighting. It was a curtain which helped him to shut out more completely the world with its many perplexities and the ties of the heart. . . ."[6] Because of the music in his mind, Beethoven said, "I am never alone when I am alone."[7] Yet in a double sense, there were always human companions. He had to hope that a mass of others, present and future, would eventually cherish his music. If one did not count on their good ears, why would one publish it? One other companion was both implicit and explicit. At age fifty, as he was composing his *Missa Solemnis*, he wrote in his notebook, "God above all things. . . . For it is an eternal providence which directs omnisciently the good and evil fortunes of human beings. . . .Tranquilly will I submit myself to all vicissitudes and place my sole confidence in Thine unalterable goodness, O God. Be my rock, my light, forever my trust." Over the manuscript of the *Missa* he wrote: "Coming from my heart, may it again reach the heart."[8]

The miracle of communication between human hearts separated by time, space, and culture not only frees amateurs like me to say a word about such music but also frees music itself from elitist captivity. Great music is not only for the great. That principle comports with Beethoven's own politics, with his belief that he had more to bequeath to a future humanity than had his contemporary, Napoleon Bonaparte. A spirit deeper than politics resounds in this music. Concerning some of it, the religious among us would not hesitate to say, in words of the Apostle Paul, that in Beethoven we sometimes sense the presence of a power who speaks to us "with sighs too deep for words" (Romans 8:26).

Whether we are consciously religious or not, many of us have heard those wordless sighs. Vonnegut heard them. Music historian Steven Brown finds evidence, in ancient human culture, of communicative habits which he calls "musilanguage," an age-old fusion of sounds both musical and verbal. Parents are familiar with this language, observes Robert Bellah, in sounds which they are likely to purr lovingly over their infant children.[9]

That notion brings me back to a thirteen-year-old boy whose doorway to great music was first opened by the Beethoven Fifth. It would require another eight or ten years before I came to hear a segment of the Beethoven corpus rather removed from the vast sonic miracles of the nine symphonies. By the late 1940s, Toscanini had transcribed for string orchestra two short movements from the final string quartet, *Opus 135*. It was for me a new door into the depths of Beethoven's spirit. Over the third movement, while mortally ill, he wrote, "Song of Rest, Song of Peace." The fourth movement begins in the minor with a somber three-note tune he had picked up in a Vienna bar, "Muss es sein?" (Must it be?) Suddenly, in the major, the notes yield to a triumphant inversion: "Es muss sein!"

It was an Ode to Joy in miniature. The silences in the late quartets are as eloquent as the sounds. Many of us who make our living with talk know that the silence *between* words often anticipates or resonates with the words themselves. One waits for some words to come, some to sink in. The same applies in music. As regards Beethoven's late quartets, no other music known to me so intimately combines sound and silence or is so close to "sighs too deep for words."

Several of my friends have asked for some portions of one of those quartets to be played at their funerals. The same will do for me. It will do for many of us, because our experience of great music inclines us to agree with the last lines of Robert Browning's "Abt Vogler":

> Sorrow is hard to bear, and doubt is slow
> to clear.
> Each sufferer says his say, his scheme of the
> weal and woe.
> But God has a few of us whom he whispers in
> the ear;
> The rest may reason and welcome: 'tis we
> musicians know.

Presumptuous it may be for us amateurs to believe that we know what the musicians know. Not long after I first heard *Opus 135*, I wrote a poem, not so great as Browning's but great with gratitude to Beethoven. One of my friends of that time said, "I know that quartet, and I know what your poem means." I am sure that others will know, too.

Quartet in F Major, Number 16, Opus 135

> My fingers brush a shore of sound
> As I slip further out into the silent sea
> Which washes on the island of this noisy life.
> Oh, I have stormed the mountaintops
> And split the shells off the universe
> To free the lightning of my chords.

But time is short, and silence tugs upon my soul.
Believe me, music is the yearning of a sound to
   find a rest in soundlessness.
So what I hated most—deafened cavern for a mind—
Contents me now,
For in that silence shall I rest whence all my
   music comes.

NOTES

1 The original of this essay appeared in the journal, *ARTS:
   Twentieth Anniversary Issue*, Spring 2009. Published by
   United Theological Seminary and edited by Wilson Yates,
   46–49. Used by permission.

2 Kurt Vonnegut, *A Man Without a Country* (New York:
   Random House, 2007), 66.

3 John N. Burk, *The Life and Works of Beethoven* (New
   York: Random House,1943), 256–57.

4 Ibid., 56.

5 Ibid., 57–58.

6 Ibid., 167–68.

7 Ibid., 243.

8 Ibid., 206–7.

9 See *The Robert Bellah Reader*, ed. Steven Brown and
   Steven M. Tipton (Durham: Duke University Press,
   2006), 160.

Chapter 4

WORLD KINSHIP, LIFELONG CARE: THE CHURCH

&

"First, I thank my God through Jesus Christ for all of you, because your faith is proclaimed in all the world. For God is my witness, whom I serve with my spirit in the gospel of his Son, that without ceasing I mention you always in my prayers, asking that somehow by God's will I may now at last succeed in coming to you. For I long to see you, that I may impart to you some spiritual gift to strengthen you, that is, that we may be mutually encouraged by each other's faith, both yours and mine. I want you to know, brethren, that I have often intended to come to you (but thus far have been prevented), in order that I may reap some harvest among you as well as among the rest of the Gentiles. I am under obligation both to the Greeks and to barbarians, both to the wise and the foolish: so I am eager to preach the gospel to you also who are in Rome."

—*Romans 1:8–15, RSV*

I have a friend, a carpenter and builder, one of whose work partners asked him: "Why do you go to church?" He answered, "I want to say 'thank you' to someone."

That is as credible a beginning to a brief confession of faith in God that I know. Religious faith may not be altogether rooted in Schleiermacher's "sense of absolute dependence," but it is a good beginning. Our lives are gifts. It seems only right to offer a "thank you."

Much in American culture denies that impulse. Once in a public meeting a successful businessman said proudly, "I want you to know that I am a self-made man." To that someone in the audience responded, "If you had to do it over again, brother, wouldn't you ask for a little help?"

Fact is, we have all had more than a little. Among the species, humans spend the most years as dependent children. (How I envy those baby elephants and deer that start walking on the day of their birth!) Americans seem tempted to forget our dependencies, from conception to death. We forget in matters of religion, too. In recent years talk about religion has often involved "spirituality." Many distinguish the term from "organized religion" on the assumption that "spirit" is inherently a feature of our personal life quite apart from external relationships. Such an idea of the spiritual fits very closely to the individualism of American culture. Like the secret ballot, our inner experience of the Ultimate we deem sacred, inviolable, and altogether a matter of personal consciousness and idiosyncrasy.

To be sure, the self that is born from parents remains a unique self. Genetic science alone confirms that. Inherently dignifying is the fact that there never was, there never will be, an exact duplicate of *you*. (One needs to recover the first person singular *thou* of old English, *Du* in German, *Tu* in French.) Not even identical twins are identical; for, note the biologists, every twin has been shaped by some circumstances unique to him or her.

That admitted, our American individualism overrates the philosophy which the existentialists compressed into the adage, "Man makes himself." Oh? The facts speak otherwise. Try as some did in the late twentieth century to stress "spirituality" in contrast to "organized religion," the distinction falls afoul of ordinary daily human experience. What humans deem important, we organize: grocery stores, law courts, businesses, family picnics, gymnasiums, schools, political campaigns, churches, synagogues, and mosques.

From 2,000 years ago, the words of the Apostle Paul resonate with my own debt to the historical movement called "church." The word derives from the Greek word for "Lord" (*kurios*), suggesting that church means "the Lord's people." Every infant baptism in a church service reminds me that I, too, was once baptized as a baby. I like the significance of that event as expressed in the liturgy of the French Reformed Church.

> Little child, for you Jesus was born. For you he
> died and rose again from the dead. As yet you
> do not know anything about this. Thus we are
> assured again that "We love because God first
> loved us."

If any friend asks me why I attend worship in a location called a church, my first answer, too, would have to be: gratitude.

To document that gratitude would be virtually to write my autobiography. For eighty years, church and churches have surrounded me with testimony, encouragement, and help to personal growth without which I would not be myself. I am certain that I am not unique in this. Hoping that any who read this essay may find in it reason to recount their own debts to "organized religion," I will offer this summary from my own life.

Early and late, a congregation reminded my parents and me that there are other people who are committed to lifelong loyalty to us.

Not unique to the Christian movement, but characteristic of all the great world religions, is a commitment to care for individual members from cradle to grave. What other category of institution even tries to make good on such a claim? When it put my birth certificate in its archives, government assumed a very limited responsibility for the rest of my life. When schools bless us with knowledge of the wide world and count us as forever their (donor!) graduates, they assume no comprehensive ongoing care for the good and ill in our futures. When we resort to professional help from doctors, lawyers, and bureaucratic experts galore, they minister to only a segment of our lives. Even when the love of parents endures beyond our childhood, death destines us to be bereft of their sustaining presence. Even when we find in some friendships a loyalty and wisdom close to religious, their presence, too, can be episodic, unavailable in time of need, and snatched away by death. When we need the help of social workers, soup kitchens, and shelter for the homeless, we are likely to discover that these agencies were once invented by religiously motivated folk who felt obliged to serve parts of human life in loyalty to the whole of it.

To be a member of a Christian church is to embrace a humanistic concern for each other's lives and for all of humanity, too. We are committed to that all-embracing care inside the congregation and outside. I admire those women in our local congregation in upstate New York who sew baby clothes for infants born to women in prison; the member of our church active in the Habitat for Humanity program locally and in Central America; and the lawyer who now goes regularly to Zambia to help meet people's educational and medical needs. Then there is the struggle of our congregation to make good on its baptismal obligation to a twelve-year-old boy who suffers from a severe behavioral problem that makes him sometimes dangerous to other children. At one point the leaders of the church considered forbidding him to attend Sunday School. Finally, with much patience from the adults and with the cooperation of specialists in the community, this young man has increasingly become, in his behavior as well as in our theology, a calm and collected "child of the covenant."

Robert Frost famously said, "Home is where, when you go there, they have to take you in." True of some homes, but not of all. The Christian church is committed to the welcoming of strangers and distressed people of all sorts. In their history, churches have often failed to practice this unlimited welcome, but the church's faith stands there in judgment of the church's behavior. Among the most notorious of those failings, in the congregation of my childhood, was its implicit refusal to welcome the people of our city whom we then called Negro. Only later did this baptized Christian begin to discover this contradiction to the faith of an Apostle Paul. Time and again Paul reminded new Christians that their fellowship included a world of humans—Jews, Greeks, slave, free, men, and women. Equal access to the love of God in Jesus Christ his Lord; that was the nub of the *sociological revolution* inherent in the early Christian church. In a recent essay in *The Atlantic*, Robert Wright gives the Apostle Paul credit for the very idea of a global humanity that is actualized in hospitality to strangers all. He was a tentmaker by profession, notes Wright, and since—for travelers of the time—inns were rare and hotels non-existent, one often spent the night in one's tent by the side of the road. Thieves and murderers notwithstanding, Paul's tent gave him space for hospitality to strangers on the road. At the very least, a bona fide fellow follower of "The Way" would be welcome there, an experience duplicated in my own world travels. Connect with a church in a foreign country, and you have help on your journey. We know that in those early centuries the passport to such hospitality was not from government but from the confidence that when strangers drew the fish on the ground, they qualified as members of the Lord's people.

Every stranger was potentially qualified, that was the radical point. More passionately than the Stoics, Paul meant to build a humanity-comprehending organization, however incomplete that organization may be because of its inevitable backsliding into the forms of exclusivity that haunt every organization. The Christian movement may not be the only inventor of the notion of "humanity," but it is certainly one of them. The rationalist human rights movement of the eighteenth century was a latecomer in the matter.

If religious faith has any advantage over rationalism in pursuit of a more genuinely inclusive worldwide human community, it is the capacity of that faith for judging how we fall short of that inclusiveness in all of our institutions, including first of all the church. Paul himself wrestled with the sins of exclusivity in the daily life of those small congregations he helped plant in the Roman Empire. Judgment on one's own failures is a great test of a deep religious faith and a sturdy ethic. It is easy to condemn churches for their hypocrisies, but less easy to dismiss the phenomenon of a body of folk who, now and again, confess those hypocrisies.

The church insisted on confession of my sins and its sins, too.

In the midst of the great recession of 2009, the num
of leaders in banks, Wall Street firms, and government who
said so much as an "I'm sorry" for the worldwide losses of
trillions of dollars of supposed wealth, was minuscule. We
had plenty of leaders who explained how others deserved
the real blame.

So, the more remarkable is the existence of an institution
whose tradition invites adherents to enter a church building
and there, once a week, to confess *their* sins. As a longtime
Protestant, I know the distortions of bad conscience that
disable one from the joys of thanksgiving. I know how
narrowly we sometimes define "sin" and how apt we are
to think "sex" when we think sin with nary a thought for
whether war or being in a business that loans poor people
money at 30 percent interest is a sin. Some versions of
Protestantism are so emphatic on asserting "the guilt and
power of sin" that when the gospel of forgiveness and
"renewal of life" finally enters the sermon, the congregation
cannot believe in the gospel because they are so drowned
in the guilt. Nonetheless, the church is almost the only
organization that takes the concept of sin seriously.

Publicly and privately, the word "sin" is harder to utter
than the word "evil." Sin assumes human responsibility,
personal and public. In 2009, Harvard historian Niall
Fergusson published a book, *The Ascent of Money*,
which *The New York Times Book Review* described as
"a heartbreaking . . . survey of human evil." A New York
minister who read the review was among the few people in
our city to speak about the 2008–2009 recession in words
like these.[1]

> Most would agree that if a change of course
> is called for, it is not simply incumbent upon
> "them," be they Wall Street, the mortgage
> industry, careless borrowers, Congress or
> financial regulators. Rather [a] course change

bent upon every one of us, caught as
e in that skein of sin that this
l crisis has so cruelly and accurately
d back on us.[2]

ispensable private and public language for
dea____ he phenomenon of evil in human history,
past and present. Not just evil out there, but evil in here.
I learned to speak and to understand that language in the
church. My sin contributes to humanity's, and it to mine. It
is an uncomfortable doctrine. Nobody who goes to church
regularly should expect on every Sunday to be comforted.
A perturbed spirit is sometimes the result of being touched
by the Holy Spirit.

*The church has often called me to combat the evils of
society that suffuse the church itself.*

Back in 1962, as local violence erupted around the
attempt of an African-American named James Meredith
to enter the law school of the University of Mississippi, a
Presbyterian minister named Robert Walkup recounted to
his congregation in nearby Starkville a story from his own
childhood: how, in reaction to the murder of a black man,
the local legal officials chose to ignore the crime. What's the
best word for describing that event? he asked. "It was *sin* . . .
I'm his grandson, and I'm paying for that sin and the sins of
others who were silent."

Such theological language, applied to racism, was
only too rare in the church pulpits of that time. But in my
own case, a church service launched me at age twenty on
a pilgrimage toward repentance that no child of a black
family ever joined my family in that baptismal ritual in a
church in the 1930s.

For me, the occasion for racial repentence was a
conference for young people in western North Carolina in
the summer of 1948. It was the first time in my life when
I sat at a Communion table in the company of African-

American peers, and the first presided over by an African-American minister, Lucius Pitts. During the week of the conference, he had carefully shared with us some of the struggles of southern black people to survive the terrors of a segregated, discriminating society. In the communion service, as he intoned the benediction, "brothers and sisters, go in peace," something had happened to me beyond mere knowledge that something terribly wrong had been done to the black people of American society. I had participated in a meeting of white and black people around a table prepared long ago as a door into a different kind of society. It was not to be the first time when I would become aware of an evil in an occasion that promised deliverance from it. Sometimes an announcement of forgiveness prompts one to confess that we have sins needing forgiveness.

A large part of my life during the next sixty years would involve struggle with myself and with others over how to overcome racism in America and the world. As I went to that meeting in western North Carolina, I was already a student at nearby Davidson College, where not one of my fellows was black but where one was a young German, Dieter Oberndoerfer. He was to become a distinguished professor of political science. He had scarcely survived Hitler's "war against the Jews." Like me, he became aware of the poison of racism in American as well as in German history. Like me and other white Christians—like the colleges, congregations, and assorted racism-beset institutions of America—we needed the help of forces outside the bounds of organized religion in order to grow in awareness of the true evil of the thing. Perhaps Germans needed their defeat in World War II; perhaps we Southerners needed our defeat in the Civil War, to realize the evils of racism. Without doubt, we needed the help of law and public protest movements for exorcizing it from our personal souls and our social body.

Like me, Martin Luther King, Jr. was still in school

in 1948. But something churchly, something spiritual, something transcending custom was at work in the land and in the selfhood of us both. I came to owe the Civil Rights Movement and the work of black scholars a great debt for raising my consciousness and conscience about racism. But to special segments of the church I owe the real beginnings of it all.

Doing the truth: peer group help and the help of being asked to do what you were not sure you could do.

Perhaps the real beginning of my appreciation for the church was earlier, when, as a fifteen-year-old, I joined a local Presbyterian church and went regularly to its Sunday evening youth group. My ultimate debts to that group were twofold. Its members were something of a little church inside the big one (*ecclesiola in ecclesia*). We were partners in youthful struggles with growing up—social identity, sex, work-to-be, and religious faith. We hear much about "peer group pressure" and the erring ways of the young. But there are benign peer pressures, such as I knew in that youth group.

It was in fact my start on a road that would take me to many a summer conference and to that prejudice-breaking occasion in 1948 in North Carolina. Twenty years later, in the midst of the momentous conflicts of the 1960s, a number of Protestant denominations abandoned their formally organized programs for high school and college-age members, often at the behest of the latter who asked for acknowledgment as full members of the church, not junior members. It was a great mistake. In my generation, many of us became convinced Christians under the influence of a youth movement within the church. Almost all of the adult leaders who were our advisers in that movement are dead now. I have often mourned that fact, for I have wanted to say "thank you" to them for the hopes they nourished in us by paying attention to our needs as young people. In

On Second Thought

no small measure, their presence was our link to the larger church, and they were our models for becoming models to a future generation of the young.

Their influence became powerful not only from linking us to a broad spectrum of official church leaders. It came also when, *mirabile dictu*, they asked us to try being one of the leaders. At the start it could be a threatening invitation. Many adults shy away from speaking in public because they never were asked to do so. Many shy away from voicing their doubts about politics and religion, for they fear controversy. An athletic, musical, writing or speaking ability remains dormant in many a person because no one has ever asked them to exercise it. Even if we know we have such ability, the refusal of peers to acknowledge that can discourage the young. My wife Peggy transferred into a new school system for eighth grade. After her attempts to do well in this or that assignment, such as giving an oral book report, other students greeted her with such perceived hostility (ah, the eighth grade!) that she became fearful of speaking before the class. By contrast, in the local church youth group she found freedom of expression and a spirit of mutual appreciation that liberated her to exercise her gift for putting thought into words.

I compare that experience to historical accounts of how the early Wesleyan movement in Wales, in their "classes" of twelve members, gave to Welsh coalminers their first opportunity to exercise some leadership in matters religious and political. From that experience, some of those early Methodists laid one foundation of the British Labor Party, without much benefit from the rise of Marxist communism.

Young people need opportunity to try their wings without the danger of falling flat. I still remember a moment after a short meditation on a certain passage of the Bible when the adult adviser said quietly to me, "You have the making of a fine teacher." I also remember volunteering to sketch the life of the Apostle Paul for a Sunday evening youth group. Surely none of my peers from that group remembers that presentation; but I do, just as every member of a graduate school seminar is most likely to remember what she or he said in discussion of the day's topic. Here appeared in my own early life an educational principle "more honored in the breach than in th'observance" in much of my own upbringing in schools: the *responses* of students to the teaching cements the lesson in the minds of the students themselves.

The phrase that encapsulates the principle for me is from the New Testament: "doing the truth." The philosophy called pragmatism outflanks many other versions of learning on this point. It is common wisdom among academics that "if you want to learn something, try teaching it." Professionals in every field know that practice may not make perfect—only good practice makes perfect—but one's grasp of a book deepens when one tries to offer to others what the book means to oneself. Social psychologist Kurt Lewin was right when he said, "Nothing is so practical as a good theory." But one can only be sure that it is a good theory after one has put it into practice. No one trusts a doctor who has never experienced an internship. The same applies to us who dare to undertake professions related to the church and religion. Theology takes us into new levels of awareness after we have to talk to a dying church member, a grieving widow, or a young person who wonders about suicide. Academics become more than theoretical when we observe students ruminating on the conflict between making money and serving human need in their own choice of a profession. We teachers explore the conflict in a lecture; they carry it on into their lives. We both discover the deepest human truth when we try to *do* it.

I thank God for all those ministers, teachers, advisers, and friends—most of them in the context of churchly affairs—who offered me not only their versions of "truth" but also opportunity to test out my own versions in public talk, in the design of a project, in experiments of collaboration with other human beings. A scientist friend of mine once commented that his wife's resistance to religion stemmed from the fact that in her youth religion was "fed to her like spinach." Quite different was my experience of religious mentors in the church. They taught, they preached, they suggested books. But they left me room to ruminate, to chew, and to discover if spinach or some other nourishing dish was to my taste. It was a whiff of democracy in the intellectual-spiritual life of some churches. It was good education. Above all, it was good religion.

A door to the world.

More than most, I was fortunate to be invited by the church to experience its worldwide presence in dozens of countries. But the seeds of that experience had many a local sprout, thanks to those kindred of Paul who built the network of congregations that embodied the church-ecumenical. Scholars say that the twentieth century ecumenical movement had two powerful roots: the foreign missionary movement and inter-confessional study of the Bible. Missionaries to India and the Congo discovered that the western denominational divisions of churches made little sense to village farmers. Simultaneously, the academic study of the Bible began to cross those divisions. The Bible was the common authority for all the churches; why not, in one Bible, an invitation to oneness among the churches?

My lifetime saw the churches of the world coming home, in a reversal of the missionary movement, to the locales of America. In my little church in Gastonia, North Carolina, the local newspaper did not feature much foreign news. But in occasional visits of a Christian from across the seas, their country and their church became personally real to us locally. Their visit made real, too, the ecumenical vision of the Apostles who founded those early Christian churches. Long before the internet, air travel, and television brought the lives and deaths of our world neighbors into our daily awareness, the great world religions were already proclaiming the kinship of human folk worldwide. None of the religions promoted this kinship, in principle and in action, more vigorously than the modern Christian churches.

Among many other experiences of that astonishing world church, one from Zimbabwe sticks in my memory. There we were in a small rural town, invited to sit in on an all-night meeting of the locally grown congregation of one of Africa's "new" churches. The claim was that the Holy Spirit had planted this congregation, not a western missionary. The Spirit did not plant it, however, without the Bible. There in a large public place was a young man reading from the Bible, verse-by-verse, as a blind elder leader preached his interpretations, verse-by-verse. That worship service went on all night. It aimed at an early morning climax in baptisms in the village river. It was not the Sunday church service to which I was accustomed. But there was that Bible, there the preacher, and there the preparation of a baptism, coterminous and consistent with the pioneering theological and missionary work of the ancient apostles.

The church worldwide is a great human and humanizing community. Or such has been my principal experience of it. Once on a Sunday in Indonesia, our World Council of Churches hosts arranged for our visiting committee members a chance to spend Sunday morning with upcountry local congregations. One of them, way up the mountain and in the midst of small farms, welcomed Peggy and me. As part of that welcome, the leaders asked me, via translator, to speak a bit about myself and my reason for being in Indonesia. Offering a five-minute sketch, I was about to sit down when a certain agitation went through the small congregation. Said my translator: "They want to know about your family." Of course! What is more common to all of us worldwide than the marriages that gave us birth, that produced our children, and that have shaped our lives in a thousand ways daily? Afterward, it reminded me of Bonhoeffer's image of "Christ existing as community," as an assembly of human beings who care for each other's troubles, joys, sorrows, hopes and loves, ". . . that we may be mutually encouraged by each other's faith. . . . " That experience, so real in the life of Paul and his scattered little church communities, came replicated into my life twenty centuries later. Not to rejoice in the enormous privilege of belonging to such a global community is to suffer spiritual shrinkage.

Among other gifts from that global Christian community are the people whose names and faces enrich my images of their respective countries with particularity, friendship, and personal connection. For me, 700,000 villages in India are not just a statistic. One of them is the place where I talked with a small group of discouraged Christians pleased to hear about my own new awareness of Christians throughout India. South Korea is not simply the place where three of my college classmates died in a war; it is also the place where Dr. David Kwang-sun Suh and dozens of other graduates of Union Seminary struggled against the dictatorships of 1960–90, who went to prison for that cause, and who by email still keep me aware of the imperial presence of America in their country.

Similarly for me, South Africa is not merely a place where five million white people dominated the lives of thirty million black people in a system called apartheid. It is also the place where Desmond Tutu, Beyers Naude, Peter Storey, Ginn Fourie, Alex and Jenny Boraine, John

DeGruchy, Charles Villa-Vicencio, and Joe Seramane fought that system. It is also a township named Tembisa on the outskirts of Johannesburg, one of whose families gave me dinner and a bed to sleep in one night in 1992, impressing on my memory forever the fact that poverty is no barrier to hospitality in Africa. Germany is not only the country which gave birth to Nazism and the murder of six million Jews. It is also repentant post-war Germans who celebrate the fidelity of Dietrich Bonhoeffer, who are educating their children and grandchildren to know what evil is and how to resist it, and who are personified in my life by Richard von Weizsaecker, Helmut and Erica Reihlen, Eberhard and Renate Bethge, Geiko and Helga Mueller-Fahrenholz, and Albrecht Schoenherr.

I will always believe in an assembly of human beings named the Communion of Saints. I have known a few of them. They are a great global gathering. They have done me the favor of suggesting that I belong to their company. It is legion.

The Church fortifies hope. It asserts our Creator's intention to save us humans in spite of ourselves and our histories.

In the fall of 2004 I happened to be in a living room conversation with a small group of German Christians. I rehearsed my sense, as an American citizen, of being betrayed by the military adventures of our Bush administration and its attacks on law and human rights that supposedly constitute the American political tradition. To this liturgy of political malaise, my German friends made reply: "We agree that these are troubling developments, but we are sure that American democracy has great resources for self-correction. Just wait. Bush and company will get corrected."

What irony, I later reflected. Here were Germans with memories of Nazism, citizens of a new democratic Germany, urging Americans to have faith in their own system. It was persuasive tonic to my despair. The election of Barack Obama in 2008 brought cheers from my German friends. It confirmed for them what they had said to me in 2004.

Nonetheless, when probed, they would agree that the future of the human race must not be trusted to the hands of a political system. They know only too painfully how voters helped put Hitler into power, and how—so long as Nazi policies seemed successful—huge crowds of Germans saluted the swastika and trusted the military to secure a "thousand-year Reich." Millennia ago, Plato observed how a society can decline swiftly from democracy to dictatorship. The decline of the Weimar Republic of the 1920s echoed his analysis.

Popular thinking tends to identify democracy with majority rule. Better, I think, to identify it with personal rights and minority freedoms. Trusting majorities eventually to "get it right" defies some sobering examples of majorities that got "it" very wrong. A majority of southern white people in the 1830s settled into support of slavery in the wake of the failures of local anti-slavery societies to persuade state legislatures to get rid of an evil that was too profitable to get rid of. Instead, there persisted lonely voices like that of Adelaide and Sarah Grimke of South Carolina. Sarah wrote a book, documented with passages from the Bible, that brought plantation slavery under the judgment of God. For her trouble, South Carolina was glad to see her exiled to Philadelphia. Late in the nineteenth century, under the slogan, "We are God's chosen people," Albert Beveridge carried most Americans with him in his colonialist vision for America in the coming twentieth century. William Graham Sumner's warning against this "grand onslaught on democracy" did not prevent Beveridge's election as U.S. senator from Indiana.

My German friends may be right: the slow retreat from bad policies, supported by majorities, sometimes comes from the diligent efforts of minorities. In the meantime. great human suffering may have come, the self-correcting of democracy having come too late.

If it comes at all, a minority—sometimes a minority of one—has usually done its unpopular work. The biblical histories of Israel and the young church are replete with illustrations. From Nathan, the public critic of King David, to Jeremiah, the scourge of misdirected Judean patriotism, the speaking of hard truth has often fallen to small minorities of prophets and their friends.

And that is largely true, from 30 A.D. to 2009 A.D., in the struggle of Christian churches over issues of justice and truth in their own internal affairs and their public witness. Martyrdom-vulnerable early Christians had to keep on insisting that "Jesus Christ is Lord" while the majority of Roman citizenry assured Jesus-people that there was no harm to paying homage to the bust of Caesar in every town square. No doubt many church members joined that consensus, just as a majority of American church members are inclined to support any war which a government decides is "just." Sometimes a church minority has to practice a Gospel-ethic until the majority finally agrees that they were wrong. Finally, most white Christians in South Carolina had to agree that Sarah Grimke was right.

When it comes to the contribution of Christians to my hope for the future of our human species, my case rests on the record of certain minority witnesses in Germany, South Africa, China, Korea, and Japan. In Nazi Germany a small coterie of religious and secular citizens hid Jews, plotted to help Jews escape from Germany, preached against Nazism from pulpits, joined the resistance, went to concentration camps, and got executed. From this heroic minority, some of whom protested on grounds of religious conviction, it is possible to derive some vigorous hope for the future of our humanity. It is not a hope based on elections.

The case from South Africa is a little different and somewhat more hopeful. Unlike Hitler, the architects of racist policies in pre- and post-1948 South Africa professed Christian faith. Their government never banned churches, only individuals and institutions that insisted on reading the Bible as antagonistic to the basic idea of apartheid. Large majorities of South African whites applauded apartheid, especially in the Dutch Reformed Church, closest of ecclesiastical partners to the government. But then there was Beyers Naudé: practicing orthodox theologian, who was offered the most prestigious of all pulpits in the DRC, who refused to support apartheid policies on theological grounds, who was stripped of his ordination, and confined for years to the privacy of home, but who yet exercised public leadership as ally of black churches and black liberation. Finally Naudé was vindicated and welcomed back in the 1990s into the ministry of a DRC repentant for apartheid and for its treatment of him thirty years before.

I remember a Sunday morning in Johannesburg when Beyers took us to the small church in the Alexandria township where he shared ministry with a black colleague. Afterward, he toured the neighborhood with us. He showed us the huge array of apartments for mine workers living far from their homes to the south. As we walked and talked with neighbors, down those dusty streets and past those shaky shacks, I was sure that we were in the company of a saint.

Like all human selves, saints require company. Desmond Tutu, Peter Storey, Nelson Mandela, and hundreds of others accompanied Beyers Naudé in his trek of opposition to racism. The Christians in that company were many, but secularists and they together formed a body of protesters who, joined by forces outside of South Africa, finally effected one of the world's historic examples of a relatively peaceful political revolution.

The Christians of China offer another example, only tangentially political. Two large segments of believers in modern China—the house churches, and the government-legitimated congregations of the China Christian Council—are proof of the persistence of faith and church in that country. During the Cultural Revolution (1966–76), the leader of the C.C.C.—Bishop K.H. Ting—found himself forcibly exiled from his academic and church post into the life of a peasant farmer. He and thousands of other Christians emerged from that political attempt to kill religion in China to become builders of China's major Protestant churches. They developed the country's largest theological seminary in Nanjing. With a leader of the Buddhist community, Ting succeeded in getting the government to include a mandate for religious freedom in the text of the People's Republic's new constitution. Like defenders of the church in East Germany, K. H. Ting cooperated with a Communist government for the sake of protecting the integrity and existence of the church in China.

The other side of Christianity in modern China took a different track. In 1987, and again in 1999, village "house churches" welcomed us visiting Protestants. Technically illegal and closely watched by the government, these small congregations are the persisting legacies of western missionary witness in the nineteenth and early twentieth century. As one listened to the hymns sung in these informal Sunday worship services, the tunes and the translated verses echoed the witness of missionaries in the 1930s. A throwback into history, yes, but it was also a witness to the endurance of a faithful congregation across two generations of political repression. During the Cultural Revolution, we are told, Christians practiced Tai Chi in the public parks and quietly prayed with each other under that disguise. During the ten years of the Cultural Revolution, living room prayer meetings sometimes hid under similar disguises. Because the missionaries had taught that every worship service should include a collection, the house church leaders took it up too. They hid the coins away in a secret jar until such time as the jar could be brought back publicly. Then there was the Hebrew biblical scholar of Nanjing seminary faculty who rescued just one copy of the Chinese Bible from flames lit by the Red Guard, only to be challenged by his wife for not rescuing two copies, "one for me too." Promptly he went to work on a new translation, which he copied out by hand over the next six or seven years.

The persecuted underground church, whose members wait for the freedom to emerge above ground, has an even more dramatic illustration in the case of the Nagasaki Catholics who went into deep hiding under the pressures of the seventeenth century Meiji revolution in Japan. During this period, the cost of a Christian's appearing in public was execution. Not until 250 years later were Christians free to appear publicly in Japan. In order to teach their children the basics of faith and worship, and to practice other strategies of survival, they persisted clandestinely for two and a half centuries, only to emerge in the mid-nineteenth century above ground.

Such segments of church history reduce me to wonder and humility. Would I be capable of that radical fidelity? Would I risk lions, burning at the stake, and life in prison for the sake of Jesus and his friends? I hope never to find out! In the meantime, these members of a church past and present are the true church for the likes of me. They witness to a faith deep, stubborn, and transcendent of government violence. Theirs is a "soft" power that proves more enduring than so-called hard power. They are the real *ecclesia*.

One other example induces wonder and humility in me. It comes from the early life of my colleague Kosuke Koyama, eminent ecumenical theologian, professor with me in the faculty of Union Theological Seminary in New York.

His mother and father were members of a small Christian congregation in Tokyo. He was twelve years old in the spring of 1942, and with the encouragement of his parents, he enrolled in a class preparing young people for full church membership. At one point in the process, the minister of the church said to him: "Kosuke, you must remember that the God and Father of Jesus loves Americans as well as the Japanese."

When one remembers that Pearl Harbor was four months past and that Japan had mobilized on every hand to fight the Americans, this was an utterly astonishing declaration of faith. Its validity was to be sorely tested three years later. Fifteen-year-old Koyama was on a Tokyo street as incendiary bombs from a thousand American planes were killing 100,000 people of that city. One bomb fell a few feet in front of him. It was a dud. He always believed that his life was saved by that "dudness." Years later, in his books and teaching, he constantly warned against confusing loyalty to country with loyalty to God and the Gospel. When, after the war and as required by the occupying American military, the Japanese emperor declared that he was not a god, a major point in the theology of a small, unpopular Japanese Christian movement finally came into political effect.

I cherish many American examples of the minorities who give me hope for the future of the human race: Moravian missionaries who resisted colossal injustices done to Native Americans in New England; Christian facilitators of the Underground Railroad; slaves on plantations who worshiped secretly in the woods and interpreted the Bible as the masters had forbidden them to do; conscientious objectors during World War II who died in greater proportion as medics than did typical infantrymen; medical doctors who have given up profitable practices to serve the sick "sans frontiers"; an Abraham Lincoln who opposed the Mexican War even though it might lead, as it did, to his defeat in the next congressional election; and four American nuns willing to die if that was the cost of serving the physical and spiritual needs of rural people in civil war-racked El Salvador in the 1980s.

T.S. Eliot wrote: "The only tragedy is not to be a saint." The church that compels my loyalty believes that sainthood is open to all sorts and conditions of us humans. It celebrates what saints do to help each other into sainthood. They are likely to spurn the designation of saint, but their behavior qualifies for it. They are not merely individuals notable for feats of piety. They are a company of the faithful who make piety real in what they do. For the sake of humanity, they "obey God rather than humans" (Acts 5:29). They live in obedience to a divine Word however much it clashes with words from human powers-that-be. They are my real heroes and heroines. They are the church that gives me hope for myself and every human on earth.

NOTES

1 Niall Fergusson, *The Ascent of Money: A Financial History of the World* (New York: The Penguin Press, 2008).

2 Michael L. Lindvall, "Course Correction," *The Christian Century*, Vol. 126, No. 15 (July 28, 2009): 27.

3 Donald W. Shriver Jr., ed., *The Unsilent South: Prophetic Preaching in Racial Crisis* (Richmond, VA: John Knox Press, 1965), 69–70.

Chapter 5

A BLESSED CONTINUITY: "RETIREMENT"

❧

few days after announcing my retirement from sixteen years as president of Union Theological Seminary in New York, the president of another seminary greeted me with the jocular question: "How does it feel to be a has-been?"

That was eighteen years ago. Long since I have known how I should have replied to him: "I don't know. I'm not dead yet."

Long since, too, I have known the differences between a job, a profession, and a vocation. Centuries ago, "professional" was not linked to an income-producing job. Nowadays, for people like me—ministers and teachers—retiring from a job can mean new freedom to practice a profession. But more: the great freedom of so-called retirement is for the further pursuit of one's vocation.

I do not envy those high-placed officers of business corporations who, as the company policy of retirement at sixty-five clicks in on some Friday, find themselves feeling bereft on the golf course on Monday. The most successful retirements are those that open up opportunities for reclaiming and expanding a vocation. In this Jimmy Carter is exemplary. I do not agree with those who see his presidency as a failure, but I do join in admiring the uses he has made of his political experience in the quarter-century since 1980. Carter's life illustrates the urgencies of a vocation.

If one is to resist the scourge of a "has been" feeling about life after retirement, however, there are some requirements. One is health; another is income enough to keep that health. My generation grew up with a government that installed Social Security and Medicare in our future, powerful programs for delivering us from the age-old burdens of poverty and poor health. Previous cultures have expected most of us to work ourselves to death. As a pastor in the textile manufacturing town of Gastonia, North Carolina, we could see every day on the streets the tired faces and slow walks of men and women who had spent thirty years as "operatives" in the industry. During most of those years, no company pension system supplemented Social Security. Not unusual were deaths of textile workers before their age of eligibility for Social Security. In 2009, as recession shrinks savings and the worth of pensions and the cost of medical care continues to escalate, millions of Americans think gloomily of the word "retirement." Politicians and economists tell us that both Social Security and Medicare are in budgetary trouble. Some ideologues describe both programs as assaults on individual initiative that should yield to trust in private insurance. A wise majority of American citizens seems not to be listening. Back in the 1930s, as my father was turning against the New Deal, little did he know that, by living to age ninety-six, he would need those secular-political forms of the Pauline ethic: "Bear one another's burdens."

The retirement situation of my American generation is uniquely troubling, however. Many of us are better off economically than our parents *and* our children. Both as family and as citizens, our times and our vocation burden us with big challenges of distributive justice. My generation is healthier and wealthier than most. Whether we are also wiser, remains to be seen.

Not neglecting the indispensability of economic and bodily requirements for a mature human being at any age, I cherish three other dimensions of wise retirements, each indebted to the spiritual foundations in the Christian faith. One concerns citizenship; a second, death; and a third, history.

Citizenship

Not often mentioned as a downside of paid employment is how, for most of us, it limits our time and energy for participating voluntarily in public life. A teacher's response to the needs of students and a minister's response to the needs of a congregation constitute basic commitments in those professions. We are paid to serve a particular group of people. But what about our neighbors who languish outside the walls of school and church? Familiar to us all is the excuse, "I'm too busy." Retirement from paid work can be a liberation from that excuse. It can give us new freedom to widen the scope of a neighborly bearing of other people's burdens. We can now attend to a neighbor's need without having to be paid. We read that, as two-job families multiply across the land, volunteers are becoming scarcer. Political parties look to paid campaign workers. Even churches cut back their weekday ministries. The good news is that college students are volunteering in growing numbers. One of the great encouraging phenomena of the 2008 national election was the entry of thousands of young people into the presidential campaign. Some had to lay aside their college and work commitments for this cause. Barack Obama owes his election chiefly to his army of young campaign workers who, at most, lived on subsistence incomes for months on end. Retirees were part of this army, too.

We all know that American society would be in yet more desperate shape if no one volunteered to serve in soup kitchens, drove voters to the polls, baked cakes for church suppers, marched in antiwar rallies, or worked with released prisoners to steer them away from a return to prison. For citizens of any age, to be free to do such things is to acknowledge a vocation for sustaining a democratic, caring society. If they have the energy, retirement from that vocation is no option for elderly Christians. The "if" is important. Two Presbyterian friends of my age say in their Christmas message: "We are busier than we can much longer permit at our age." Happy are the aged who can boast that they are "busier than ever," but not if the boast is a cloak against the realities of decline.

Finitude and Gratitude

A retirement discipline requires more than activity. Things more inward and contemplative must come to the fore, especially if we are to resist two powerful promptings of late-life despair: our finitude, that will climax in death, and our worry over the future of our species. The great finitude is our oncoming death, a certainty that activism can sometimes obscure. The old medieval discipline of *memento mori* is wise for any age. Once, a grandchild of three reminded us at a dinner table: "You are going to die. I am, too." How she became aware of death, I do not know. It was a precocious awareness from which some parents want to protect their young. In our mobile society that separates the generations, some young people grow to thirty without having to attend a funeral of a relative. The body of my grandmother in her casket is among my most vivid memories from my tenth year, along with the grief of my father who knew that among her five sons his mother always had a special affection for him.

When one reaches retirement age, the death of people who have enriched our lives begin to accumulate. It is one of the great burdens of old age. Early and late, death is the great "subtractor." It takes away people we loved most; and, like the image of a great tree falling in Sandburg's sorrow at Lincoln's death, they leave behind "an empty space against the sky." John Donne famously said that "every death diminishes me by one," a fact that becomes personal in the death of family and friends. As friends and colleagues die, one loses all opportunity for writing a letter or picking up the phone to ask them, "How do you feel about . . . ?" The subtraction of wife and friends from his life left my father ambivalent about living to ninety-six. "They are all gone," he said sadly.

Can anything lift the burden of such deprivation? Young optimists say, "Make new friends. Keep living. Keep your eyes on the future." For a certain Protestant conscience—I know it well—"has been" likes to bow to "yet-to-be." Optimistic Robert Browning invited his beloved to "grow old along with me" believing that "the best of life is yet to be." Browning may be too optimistic; most of us over-eighties have to concede our age. The past may have held the best, and one's enjoyment of retirement is time to remember it. Contemporary conversation dismisses the past flippantly with the remark, "It's history." In that remark, we allocate the past to unreality, and thus we allocate each other to history as to a dustbin.

When others around us die, we become surer that death

is our destiny, too. There is something immeasurably sad about the deaths of the able, accomplished, loving people who have been partners in one's life history from decades ago. One wants to complain to God: Why did you waste those wonderful lives by letting them die so soon? Why were Schubert, Mozart, Mendelsohn, Bonhoeffer, and Martin Luther King, Jr. never allowed to live beyond their thirty-ninth year?

A great antidote to the despair in this grief is systematic, disciplined gratitude for the living and the dead whose existence has blessed us. Taking time to identify gratefully the contributions to one's life by others, before they die, can be balm from Gilead. In a final note to me when he was not far from death, Episcopal bishop Paul Moore responded gently to my note to him, "Yes, we have done a few things." He had done more than a few. He deserved lots of gratitude. Beyers Naudé of South Africa lived long enough to hear belated tributes to his sacrifices on behalf of abolishing apartheid from his church and his country. Well that some of us pursue our calling to "do justice" whether or not anyone offers gratitude for our efforts; but we delude ourselves if we pretend that we have not been sustained, from time to time, by many "thank yous" that can come our way. When a student tells you, "I have never forgotten the day in class when you said . . ." or a parishioner recalls a gesture of ministry which we had quite forgotten, we cherish our own pasts with a new joy. One of the most precious of my memories of being a local church pastor was a phone call thirty years after my three short years in that position. On the line was the husband of a woman who had been a mainstay of our small congregation in western North Carolina. She had directed the choir and—for years when our denomination had just begun to ordain women as "ruling elders"—she unofficially filled that office in ways that church women have undertaken from time immemorial. The husband on the phone relayed her request: "Eleanor is dying, and she wonders if you would have a prayer with her by phone." Stumbling to meet that awesome request, I offered prayer on her behalf to the One in whom we live and die and have our being. It was the enormous privilege which pastors are likely to inherit from time to time. Unlike almost every other profession, the minister, rabbi, and priest are custodians of care for others at their birth, at their death, and across the years in between. From some of these caring relationships, there is the blessedness of no retirement.

The hearts of Christians in the ancient church in Philippi must have warmed when, in the first sentence of his letter to them, Paul exclaimed, "I thank God in all my remembrance of you" (Philippians 1:3). We Protestants gave up praying for the souls of the dead, but we should not give up our prayers of gratitude for the dead, hence the importance of All Saints Day in our annual liturgies. Often in letters to friends who share a mutual grief at the death of one we both loved, I quote those words of the Apostle. They stand at the head of his letter in some tension with words he writes three chapters later: ". . . forgetting what is behind me, and reaching out for that which lies ahead, I press forward. . . ." (Philippians 3:13–14, NEB). The disposition of most Protestants, myself included, is to take these words so seriously that we sit lightly on remembering and valuing "what is behind." Our American culture encourages this neglect, as historian Carl Becker noted when he imaged our cultural preference for the future as vehicle passengers who always look ahead, who consider the past as so much dust kicked up in the rear. This disposition can incline one to dismiss our own life works in deference to the danger of overweening pride in them. At times I am sure that some worthwhile achievements in my life should have moved me to the prayer, "Thank you, Lord, for empowering me to do that."

Doubtless one's yearning to know that others have indeed benefitted from one's lifework has its own temptation. One protection from such temptation in the discipline of counting blessings which came not only from "what the Lord has done" (as the old hymn has it) but also from what other humans have done. We may doubt our contributions to others; there is no doubt about their contribution to us. One is likely to remember those contributions belatedly upon learning of the death of a friend. "Oh, I never thanked her for what she meant to me." One lesson there: try overt gratitude before she or he dies. Write them a letter out of the blue. Append a personal P.S. to a Christmas card. Surprise them.

When we think about it, we who call ourselves Christians have in common with almost all religiously minded people a set of human debts to generations long departed from the earthly scene. Some debts are cultural: to inventors of our languages, our institutions, our libraries, our art, and our scriptures. The Maori of New Zealand, unlike most Westerners, do not march into the future face-forward. They back into it, eyes on the past, keeping a distance from it out of respect for it—as one backs away from royalty. To think, remember, and pray about pasts—recent or long distant—is to sharpen our awareness that a vast company of other humans have nourished us into all our years. They nourish us into death, too. They have given us daily reason to thank our Great Creator for all of them, living and dead. Jesus reminded his disciples that "others toiled and you have come in for the harvest of their toil" (John 4:38). The Apostle Paul echoed that wisdom when he exclaimed to fractious, pride-inflated Corinthian congregants, "What do you possess that was not given you? If then you really received it all as a gift, why take the credit to yourself" (I Corinthians 4:7)? Like many truths which come down to us in religious clothing, this one has an empirical base. Whoever grew up without a lot of help?

Becoming a helper in turn is a regular practice of real human maturity. Some years ago a distinguished psychiatrist spoke in Raleigh, North Carolina. Commenting on mental health, he said: "One of the great principles of mental health is getting involved in the lives of other people. Someone said, 'Whoever would save his life will lose it; and whoever loses his life will save it.' I forget who said that, but it is a great principle."

Members of my profession make it our business to remind our constituents as to who said that and who inserted the words "for my sake" (Luke 9:24)! Jesus himself might have agreed with the wisdom, "You can do a lot of good in the world if you don't care who gets the credit." But he knew that ingratitude was a deep spiritual fault. He said as much when he marveled that only one of ten lepers healed by him came back to "give praise to God" (Luke 17:11–19).

Giving some credit, including to oneself, can be a service to truth. One of the great promises of the New Testament is that everyone will encounter in the Last Judgment the greatest of all congratulations: "Well done, good and faithful servant. . . . Enter into the joy of your master" (Matthew 25:21). Rather neglected, I suspect, is the mystery of God's own joy and pain over what humans do and do not do. It is said that, on his deathbed at age forty-two, Thomas Aquinas gestured to the shelf of his writings and exclaimed, "Straw." I hope that the deity soon disagreed. Aquinas could not know how valued his books would be to future theologians, Catholic and otherwise. Perhaps he should have accorded to God the joy of anything well done by humans, including theology. Mighty divine works cast human books in the shade, but Bach had it right when he believed that human works can call attention to the glory of God, just as Calvinists had it right when they began one of their catechisms with the sentence, "The chief end of humanity is to glorify God and enjoy God forever." Might God have an intention of enjoying his/her creatures forever? Genesis 1:31 suggests as much. The Creator looked at those mighty works and exclaimed, "Very good." "Joy in heaven" complements and transfigures joys on earth. Imagine this height of human achievement: giving joy to the great Creator of the universe. The sturdy young Scottish athlete Eric Liddell, as played by Hugh Hudson in the film *Chariots of Fire*, had absorbed this doctrine in his Presbyterian upbringing: "It pleasures God when I run well!"

Maybe even Bach overdid the "solus" in *soli Dei Gloria*. The late Lewis Thomas, the great medical pioneer in the treatment of cancer, asked what proud achievements we humans might choose to broadcast to fellow creatures in other starry places. We would do well, he suggested, to choose the music of Bach. "We would be bragging, of course."[1] Perhaps some things in human history give both our species and our Creator bragging rights.

History and Hope

In the Hindu tradition, a man spends the first twenty years or so of his life in education, broadly defined. In the next twenty-five, he devotes himself to work and family. Finally, at age fifty, he leaves work and family for the solitude of the forest, hoping to acquire wisdom that prepares him for death. I am not sure how Hinduism deals with the ethics of leaving wife and extended family to shift for themselves, but I am sure that retirement years offer the opportunity to ponder great, perennial questions about the meaning, worth, and future of human life on this planet. Happy are retirement years blessed with the continuing presence of wife, husband, visits from children and grandchildren. Happy also are those quiet hours in which one can entertain thoughts about the whole of one's years and the years of others who, one hopes, will outlive oneself. One does not need a lonely forest refuge to ponder these great questions. Indeed, to choose no companions for this task is to forget a truth which fifty years of life ought to teach anyone: good thinking requires good companions. As a writer, I agree with the woman in one of E. M. Forrester's novels who remarks, "How do I know what I think until I hear what I say?" I prefer a variation of that: "How do I know what I should think until I hear what you say?"

When the French philosopher Descartes shut himself up in a stove for a day to ponder undeniable truth, he lighted on the principle, *cogito ergo sum*. Genesis 2:18 portrays a more likely Creator-wisdom: "It is not good for the man to be alone." Marriage has enriched my particular life beyond my describing of it. It has validated this "not good" every day now for fifty-six years. We two think our best thoughts when we have put them through the sieve of shared conversation. No wonder that a Catholic friend remarked in one of her public lectures decades ago, "I used to think that marriage was chiefly for reproduction. I now think it is chiefly for conversation."

Frequently now, in that ongoing conversation, Peggy and I give ourselves time to think on hopes and worries about a human future which we will not live to see. A certain uselessness there may be to spend diminishing days on earth preoccupied with questions that are up to future generations to answer. Yet the young have a right to ask the "retired" among us to ponder what sort of future our pasts impel us to hope for them in years that we will not live to see.

If they were to ask, I would commend to them two prime hopes that my own eighty-two years mandate for that future: (1) That we humans will do our part to save this earth from our species' assault on other species, and (2) that we will find ways to overcome our propensities for violence against our own kind.

Ecological and human violence have so expanded in the twentieth century that our young successors might well ask what we did to lessen the weight of this history that now burdens theirs. I am sure that the older generation of the twentieth century has no monopoly on telling how the people of the twenty-first century should live. But the ultimates of our species' life and death need conversation between the old and the young. One attempt to contribute to that conversation is the last essay in this collection. For the moment, here are a few yearning thoughts about our human propensity for violence.

A few years ago, I had the task of addressing an all-Jewish audience on the theology of Abraham Joshua Heschel. As coincidence had it, just five days before I was in the country of Heschel's birth, Poland. I had then made my first visit to Auschwitz and Birkenau. Unable to sleep in early morning hours back in the hotel, I had read many pages of Heschel's great work, *The Prophets*. I will never forget his definition of the prophet.

> The prophet is a person who suffers
> the harms done to others. Wherever
> a crime is committed, it is as if the prophet
> were the victim and the prey.
> All prophecy is one great exclamation; God is
> not indifferent to evil. He is always
> concerned. He is personally affected by what
> man does to man. He is a God of pathos.
> This is one of the meanings of the anger of
> God: the end of indifference.[2]

With images of Auschwitz and echoes of Heschel ringing between my ears, I came the following week to the Jewish Theological Seminary in New York. I looked out on that audience painfully aware that virtually every person there was living a life touched by the horrors of the Holocaust: fathers, mothers, grandparents, uncles, aunts, nieces, nephews, friends, and colleagues—all consumed in an evil version of "whole burnt offering," served up to twentieth century history as its prime example of human contempt for fellow humans. When one speaks to the survivors of such horror, what does one say? Saying nothing, just respectful silence, may be best. As one follows the Auschwitz guide into this and that room of the camp museum, as one looks at the bins of suitcases, human hair, eyeglasses, toothbrushes, she says, "Try to remember that a human hand once held this luggage, that human eyes once looked out through these glasses." The group she is guiding can only respond with awed silence.

A former chancellor of the Jewish Theological Seminary once commented to me, "There is no such thing as Holocaust theology." The Devil is a bad theological teacher. The ultimate devilish temptation posed by Auschwitz is this: is it any longer possible to believe in the God of Abraham, Isaac, Jacob, and Jesus? Psalm 139 asked the rhetorical question, "Whither can I escape from thy spirit?" For many a Jew and Christian in my century, the atheistic answer was: "Auschwitz." In the nineteenth century Nietzsche declared that "God is dead." In the twentieth century it seemed only too possible. We humans killed Him.

Jews now see that the survival of any Jew in the face of Hitler's evil intentions is itself a victory over evil. They also see the postwar formation of the state of Israel as part of that victory. The deepest, incomparably ironic victory of Nazism, many believe, would be the disappearance of faith in the Power who brought a people out of Egyptian slavery and—Christians add—blocked the crucifying power of Rome with a resurrection. The last, tragic success of the Nazi intent would be the abolition of all the faith of all the children of Abraham. Can that faith survive Auschwitz and all its imitations in subsequent history? That night at JTS I had come to believe that the question presses upon

Christians as heavily as upon Jews. Christians need the help of Jews for modern answers to the question. So, remembering Heschel, I made to that audience two proposals:

"If Jews, after Auschwitz, can believe in God, then Christians might, too."

"If God, after Auschwitz, can believe in us humans, then we might also believe in each other."

In *Night*, Elie Wiesel's 1957 memorial of his own months as an adolescent in that earth-version of hell, he offered one slim, hopeful assertion of faith in the divine spirit in the midst of the horrors. It is an incident widely quoted now by Christians hungry for some answers to the agony of "Where was the God of Israel in Auschwitz?"

A ten-year-old boy was being hanged. His slight weight prolonged his dying. "Where is your God now?" whispered one inmate to another. The answer, wrote Wiesel, had to be: "Here He is. He is hanging here on this gallows."[3] Christians believe that assertion. It replicates for us the truth of the cross of Jesus. Such slight glimmers of light in the night of Auschwitz, however, will remain very slim if we who honor Jesus as God's self-revelation lack the fortifying faith of twenty-first century Jews who, against much intimidating evidence, have managed to continue praying to the God of Israel. In this fortifying, we Christians have a debt to the Jewish community different from our usual assertion that Israel was God's preparation for the Good News of Jesus. Christians have traditionally advanced the notion that they have "superseded" Jews in the providence of God. The notion poses a double threat, not only to the integrity of Jews but to the integrity of Christians as well. What if Jews disappeared from earth as Nazism planned? Would Christians then disappear? Dietrich Bonhoeffer thought so. Christians in Germany, he said, have no right to intone the Gregorian chant if they are not singing it on behalf of Jews, too. The Nazi attack on Judaism was also a stalking-horse for destroying Christianity. Put most bluntly: if the God of Israel is unbelievable, then why not also the God of Jesus?

In posing that question to an assembly of my Jewish neighbors that night, five nights after my visit to Auschwitz, I joined them in a common struggle to affirm our respective paths to faith. That Jewish fidelity should be necessary for sustaining Christian fidelity is a new thought to many in both communities. In the deepest possible way, we need each other.

Whether God "exists" is a fearsome question for both. But there is another question, equally fearsome, posed by the Holocaust. In a novel written during World War II, *The Journal of Albion Moonlight*, Kenneth Patchen has a character say: The great question of the twentieth century is not, "Do we believe in God? but rather does God believe in us?"

With some 175,000,000 of us having been killed in the wars of the twentieth century, with genocidal wars proliferating into the twenty-first century, the question spills over into its corollary, "Can we believe in ourselves?" When one considers the human capacity for murdering our own kind, along with our demonstrated capacity for killing earth's ecosystem, one can be excused for thinking: "Perhaps the coming of humanity on earth was a mistake, either of evolution or of a divine Creator." What other species on earth has invented weapons capable of destroying itself and most other species in one blaze of nuclear "burnt offering"?

In his 1944 space novel, *Perelandra*, C.S. Lewis speculated on the possible new start of a human species on another planet in our solar system. In fact, the hospitality of another planet to *Homo sapiens* seems very unlikely. Various pessimists have wondered about an emigration from earth to some faraway star system via spaceship.

More optimistic is the assumption of the television series *Star Trek*; by the twenty-fourth century, the tribes of earth will have been pacified, releasing earthlings to explore the universe together.

So it goes in the imagination of "retired" Donald Shriver on a sunny day on a hillside front porch, his version of the Hindu retiree who contemplates the big questions: Is human existence, on balance, good or evil? Are we justified in loving each other? Will our capacity for hate outdo our capacity for respect, compassion, and honor for each other? And say, Mr. Shriver, whatever mandated these troubling ruminations as agenda for the ninth decade of anyone's finite earthen life?

Unfortunately, the history we have lived through mandates it. Many of us Americans in our eighties enjoy wealth, health, peace, justice, and blessings beyond-our-deserving. But to derive optimism about the human future from our particular American good luck is a momentous mistake.

After a 1991 conference on "Hate" in Norway, in an interview with Bill Moyers, Elie Wiesel's broken language resonated with a trouble that would not dissipate from his mind fifty years after his survival of Auschwitz: "Why haven't we succeeded—we who have been victims of hate—in transforming that hate into a warning? Why haven't we—that bothers me—into a warning, into a kind of alarm, saying, 'Look, look, hate means Auschwitz?'"[5] Hate leads to the belief that one neighbor or another deserves to die. Hate opens the door to the existentialist slogan, "People are no damn good." Kill them all, no matter. It bothered Wiesel. Why should it not bother every one of us, even those of us sitting on our porch on a sunny day, looking across green hillsides toward a setting sun?

Finding the significance of some whole in a small part is a rule that scientists, philosophers, and theologians each follow in their separate ways. "If it has happened once, it must be possible," said Quaker economist Kenneth Boulding. For assessing the whole of human history, the once, the twice, the many times have to be put over against the many contrary times. In the 1950s, the world of literature opened a small gate onto the horror of the Holocaust in the publication and dramatization of *The Diary of Ann Frank*. As presented on Broadway, the drama ends with Ann's father sitting in the Amsterdam attic where the family had hidden from the Gestapo. He hears a word from the diary: "I still believe that at heart human beings are good." The playwrites had alternative versions of Otto Frank's response, words for ending the play:

"She puts me to shame."

Or:

"I don't know."

There are human neighbors in our time and other times who put to shame our pessimism about our species. They are standing evidence for resisting the pessimism. We want to believe that our Creator and Preserver resists it, too. In the Bible are some precious instances when someone pleads for divine mercy for others who are undoubtedly evildoers. Abraham: Just ten "righteous" ones in Sodom, enough? (Genesis 18:32). The martyr Stephen: "Lord, do not hold this sin against them" (Acts 7:60). A dying Jesus, "Father, forgive them . . ." (Luke 23:34).

The saints are those who build the barriers against despair over the future of this hate-filled race. We need to hold on to what held them: the triumph of love over hate— not only the love that piety ascribes to God in our briefest definition of deity (1 John 4:16), but a love that persists in our own selves. Without love, the human species would not have survived until now. We have to hope that love may yet enable us to survive into far-future centuries. The saint by definition is a standing witness against despair over the past, present, and future of a race of humans who are their own worst enemies.

The Jewish and Christian traditions call us to adopt a peculiar doctrine: the God of Israel and the God of Jesus consents to become hostage in the battle between good and evil in human history: a Power not above Egyptian slavery but in it with a persecuted people, a Father not removed from the suffering of the incarnate, crucified Son but with him in that suffering. It is a dangerous, even outrageous doctrine: dangerous because even terrorists think that they are companions of God in war against evil; outrageous because, surely, a Power worth believing in must be independent of this tawdry human history. Not so, say testimonies to the God of Israel and Jesus, the God of Anne Frank, Elie Wiesel, Dietrich Bonhoeffer, and Desmond Tutu.

In the depths of the murderous struggle for and against the apartheid regime in South Africa in the 1980s, Tutu said: "In South Africa it is impossible to be optimistic. Therefore it is necessary to hope." He himself embodied that hope, as did a certain man, a political prisoner for twenty-seven years, who could have shriveled up in hatred for white people. Instead he nourished the hope in his fellow prisoners that they were on their way to being the new leaders of a new South Africa. He became its first black president: Nelson Rolihlahla Mandela. Lord, may his tribe increase.

I recommend to all retirees what I recommend to myself: Take heart for humans who will outlast us. Remember the saints. Be one if you possibly can, even in retirement.

NOTES

1 Lewis Thomas, *Lives of a Cell* (New York: Bantam Books, 1974), 53.

2 Abraham J. Heschel, *The Prophets*, Volume Two (Harper Torchbooks; New York: Harper and Row, 1962), 64.

3 Elie Wiesel, *Night* (Discus Books; Avon Books, 1969), 76

4 Kenneth Patchen, *The Journal of Albion Moonlight* (New York: New Directions Paperback, 1961), 10.

5 Public Broadcasting System, "Facing Hate with Elie Wiesel and Bill Moyers," November 27, 1991, Transcript #BMSP-19, PBS, 15–16.

Chapter 6

The Peace Education of Father and Son: 1969

❧

"How glibly we talk about 'family life,' as we do also of 'my country.' We ought to say many prayers for families. Families frighten me. May God be merciful with them."
— *George Bernanos*[1]

". . . [T]he eventual refusal of the conscripts and their families to ingest warrior values caused the Vietnam War to be abandoned. Here was evidence of how self-defeating is the effort to run in harness in the same society two mutually contradictory public codes: that of 'inalienable rights,' including life, liberty, and the pursuit of happiness, and that of total self-abnegation when strategic necessity demands it."
— *John Keegan*[2]

No decade of twentieth century American history seems more vulnerable to diverse popular images than the 1960s. Was it the decade when young Americans lost respect for institutions? For their elders? When patriotism lost out to outrage? When universities lost their educational priorities? When many young men refused to respond to the call of a young president to "bear any burden" for their country? Was it the decade of radical sexual freedom, drugs, and defiance of "the establishment"; the decade that almost destroyed the unity of the United States in a new kind of civil war? Were the 1960s the era when American defense planners invented a policy called "Mutually Assured Destruction" (MAD) with the ironic hope that it would never be implemented; or the era in which the forgotten people of democratic America— African-Americans, women, the poor, gays, and minorities galore—finally found a loud public voice? Historians prefer a quarter century to pass before they take account of an era. So histories of the 1960s now multiply. Some persons may need longer than twenty-five years, and I am one such person. I lived through the 1960s as a campus minister and faculty member at North Carolina State University. The family story to be recounted here has simmered in my memory for forty years. Seldom have I felt free to speak of these details, even to friends. Only now have I felt free to write about it all.

The gist of the story: how my family and I experienced in new ways the intimacy and the collision between local-personal and world-political events. To be sure, raised in the 1930s, I have always had reason to know that world affairs impact persons and families. My oldest uncle Alfred was wounded on the Western Front in 1918. War news was constant in the 1930s and 1940s. As a newspaper delivery boy, I followed the headlines of World War II every morning at 5 AM. Most of my male cousins, like me, were drafted into the army of that war, but all survived. Three of my college classmates in the 1950s died in the Korean War. As I grew up, it seemed natural to suppose that the United States would go to war every twenty years or so. It is a grim image of my century but, in the midst of that grimness, I led a relatively secure life. Drafted and sent to basic infantry training just after the end of WWII, I only practiced firing a gun at an enemy.

But the 1960s afflicted my life with a series of trauma that destroyed my implicit peace with the insulation of the personal from the political, the familial from the national, religious faith from world affairs.

April 1968

Many in my generation remember April 4, 1968, as a moment in which hopes for a more just American society died on a motel porch in Memphis. For some of us, more death blows came in June in a hotel in Los Angeles, again in July with police brutality in Chicago's Grant Park, and finally in November with the election of a president who promised to end the Vietnam war but whose government would take six years to do so. This string of events was accompanied daily by gritty, televised evening reports from Vietnam that fueled public suspicion that we were actually losing that war.

My most indelible memories of those awful months will always be centered on the life of our oldest child Gregory who, on April 7, 1968, was two and a half months short of his fourteenth birthday.

He was an eighth grader in a junior high school in Raleigh, North Carolina, and was one of an alternating pair of student volunteers who were assigned to raise and lower daily the American flag in the school yard. On that April 7, he lowered the flag to half-mast in mourning for the April 4 assassination of Martin Luther King, Jr. Seeing this gesture just outside his office window, the school principal, an army veteran of World War II, hurried out into the hallway and shouted the command, "Go put that flag back where it belongs."

"It already is where it belongs," muttered Gregory as the two passed each other in the hall. Infuriated, the principal raised the flag to full staff. From that moment, the school, the school system, the State of North Carolina, the Vietnam War, and fourteen-year-old Gregory Shriver were launched onto an astonishing fifteen-month course of escalating conflict.[3]

The facts of those fifteen months are not easy to summarize. For a long time, the facts were too painful for Gregory's two parents to talk about. When finally, years later, I spoke to parents of my generation about 1968–69, they usually said something like: "Yes, much the same happened to us, too."

The "same" in our family's case circled around a fourteen-year-old of considerable intellectual precocity and emotional turmoil. He exemplified the sort of student who challenges teachers to wonder: "How can I turn that churning adolescent brain and body into constructive rather than destructive directions?" Had some coterie of teachers asked that question of Gregory, his formal education might not have ended a year later. One or two of his teachers, at their own professional risk, did take him and his causes seriously. But the majority took the safer option of treating him as a problem to be suppressed rather than an opportunity for education.

For liberal parents of our generation, there will always be the rebuke of conservatives who tell us: "It's your fault. You championed the civil rights protests and the antiwar movement. You taught your children to be non-conformists. It got them into trouble. You could handle the controversies of the late 1960s. They could not." I am sure that our next-door neighbor in Raleigh talked about us this way, especially as Gregory began to advertise his politics by his hair, his dress, and the junior high project which finally did get him into trouble.

The project was an "underground" newspaper that he named *Ignition*. From the fall of 1968 into the coming spring, several friends and he wrote protests against the war, the rigidities of the public school curriculum, and the customary rote methods of public school teaching.

Meantime, the antiwar rallies rose to their 1968–69 pitch on the college campuses of the nation. Even fourteen-year-olds could identify with the protesters at Columbia, Berkeley, and hundreds of campuses in between. With the draft for them four years away (and the war seven years from ending), they had to wonder, "Is Vietnam the war of my future?" Along with thousands of his contemporaries, Gregory was determined to avoid that draft. He internalized a potent brew of reasons to protest: fear mixed with ideals, education "preparing you for your future" mixed with the threat that war could make that future very short. These many years later, he acknowledges his youthful ambivalence about the idea of military service. "Interested as I was in technology, I suspected that—once a soldier— I might yield to the lure of war machinery and even become an enthusiastic killer. It was a depressing thought."

My own 1940s generation of draftees fought the largest war in human history. To fight it, our eighteen-year-old selves had to grow up fast. We had to ponder the conflict between our family-grown ideals and the iron disciplines of an army, the waste of life on battlefields, and the division of humanity between "us" and "them." Obvious to me in infantry training was that military life requires a certain inner breakdown of civilian dispositions against killing. At eighteen, some of us had homegrown strength for internal resistance to the "slings and arrows of outrageous fortune." But the selfhood of most fourteen-year-olds lacks some of that. Precocity plus fear can make the struggle destructive and desperate. And in the 1960s, unlike the 1940s, death in combat came home every night via television and Walter Cronkite.

All this was going on while my own work as a Presbyterian campus minister at North Carolina State University brought me—and also my family—into the discussions among students and faculty about pacifism, draft refusals, and the justice-injustice of the war. Young Gregory often listened, for example on student beach retreats, to these discussions. "It was more than theory for me," he said. "It coincided with my initial adolescent coming-to-grips with death itself. And it was accompanied by my demoralizing sense of powerlessness, unfairness, and unrequited anger."

The critics of student protesters had a point about the relative immaturity of the protesters: few adolescents are ready to confront the burdens of a world in turmoil, not to speak of a world that—as in contemporary Africa—can make them orphans and then substitute-parents of siblings. Their psychological health can be much aided by a coterie of adults who empathize with their anxieties and try to protect them from their destructive impulses. However, sympathetic adults and parents are not enough to fully protect young idealists. Later in the 1990s, some American leaders would tout "family values." But in the American world of the 1960s, families could not protect their idealistic children from the massive contrary tides of other adults in schools

On Second Thought

and governments. As it happened, the school year 1968–69 found our son almost drowned by some of those tides.

During an anxious week at home watching the Democratic convention on TV in July 1968, members of our little family were caught up in the fear that a great tide of Grant Park protesters would threaten their father with the drowning. I was inside the Cow Palace as one of two elected delegates from North Carolina supporting the peace candidacy of Eugene McCarthy. As it turned out, our family's fears were groundless. Chicago police made certain of that. Not so certain, however, were the coming effects of my convention participation upon our eldest son. I was mostly thankful I had decided not to let him accompany me to Chicago. Father could pit his shoulder against the war by working inside establishments that included the university, the Democratic Party, the local city biracial committee, the local anti-poverty program, and the Southern Presbyterian Church. Sons had no such array of organizational access to world society.

But sons and daughters could join local and Washington protest marches, with or without parental permission. They could author underground school newspapers. They could dress to fit their views by keeping their hair long and wearing a father's old army uniform in the name of another mode of militancy. They could walk down the street advertising views that a parent might prudently hide behind a coat and tie.

In the spring of 1969, it was the underground newspaper which brought local media and government into the story. An issue of the paper fell into the hands of a conservative Republican television news commentator, one Jesse Helms. His daily five minute editorials on the city's major TV channel reached most of eastern and central North Carolina. Reporting on that underground paper, Mr. Helms opined: "Obviously no junior high student could write this stuff. It had to have been written by his controversial parents." It was an ambiguous compliment to the paper's real author, and an ironic slap at parents who did not use the irreverent language of a junior-high student for critiquing a war and the rigidities of public school education.

In 1969, few North Carolinians imagined that three years later Mr. Helms would get elected to the United States Senate. If he had not already been a political force in the state, his two editorials on three Shrivers could have been a media event lost in the shuffle of local news. In the meantime, copies of *Ignition* landed on desks in the North Carolina Department of Public Instruction and the state legislature downtown. Thus did a son of our household become, in some state politicians' eyes, an embodiment of the threat of student demonstrators to law and order in the land, regardless of his admiration for Martin Luther King, Jr. and his commitment to nonviolence. So far as we know, Gregory's was the first junior high underground newspaper in the state school system. Never lacking in aggressive self-confidence, Gregory managed via a student network to distribute copies of the paper to most junior and senior high schools in the Raleigh area. It was not the sort of initiative that the authorities expected from any junior high student.

In those years "protest" was often deemed by the authorities as an invitation to violence rather than an exercise of a basic democratic right. Violence did abound in the city streets of the era as well as in Vietnam. It took a lot of discipline by the student leaders of public demonstration not to be intimidated when they knew that they were no match for the armaments of the police and the National Guard. During a 1969 demonstration in Washington, Gregory took note of a line of tightly parked buses behind police barricades blocking a turn toward the White House. Curious about what lay behind the buses, he wandered behind the police line and peered between the bumpers. To his shock and dismay, he saw rows of sand bags stacked at regular intervals on the grass behind the busses. Each position was manned by uniformed soldiers armed with machine guns. In later years, he remarked on the total lack of media coverage of the government's apparent readiness to shoot students rather than let them assemble in front of the White House. That readiness would become action in the spring of 1970 with the killing of four students at Kent State University.

The multiple forces opposing student demonstrators provoked some heady misperceptions in some of these young minds. "Don't trust anyone over thirty" went their slogan, over against the fact that not all of under-thirties opposed the war, any more than all of the over-thirties supported it. All told, the times served up to the young a mix of threats fit for inducing paranoia. As Gregory was often to say later, "Just because you're paranoid, doesn't mean that no one isn't out to get you." (Maybe the whole state of North Carolina? The president of the United States? The Communists?) In his mental world, the draft board and the police were the realities that fortified paranoia. He tells how, on at least three occasions, police passed in patrol cars as he walked down the street to our suburban home. They would stop and say to him, "Hey, Shriver, what are you doing out so late?"

The most tangible reinforcement of the paranoia came a few days after the Helms editorial. Two officers of the State Bureau of Investigation came to Martin Junior High School: "We want to speak with Gregory Shriver." For an hour or so they interviewed him by himself in a room. What others helped write the newspaper? What adults did you consult with? Are you into drugs? How many demonstrations have you participated in? Why are you against the Vietnam War?

The SBI visit was illegal. The law said that police

interrogation of a fourteen-year-old must have parents present. Promptly, therefore, this father appeared in the downtown office of the state Attorney General, who admitted that his agents had acted illegally. And he added, "You know, our agents reported back saying, 'That young man is really very bright. He had some good answers to our questions.'"

That concession, however complimentary, did little to stem the onrush of near mental illness in the young man. He came home that day in a state of disconnect. It became a final blow to his ability to manage public school and public protest. The two were now going separate ways. The spring of 1969 became the last semester of formal education in the career of Gregory B. Shriver.

Tragically for him, the public school system itself collaborated with his desire to declare quits with schools. Not yet sixteen, he could not legally leave school, so the system granted him exception to the rule. Already some senior high pro-Vietnam students, via telephone, were threatening in advance to "take care of you when you get here." Counselors wondered: might not high school further upset him and him it? One got the administrative signal: "We would just as soon not have him around as a problem."

By happenstance, Gregory had a friend, a senior, at the high school to which he would be assigned. The friend overheard from an adjoining room a conversation between the principal and the boys' counselor in anticipation of Gregory's arrival in September. From that conversation and other events, Gregory described what he could anticipate in high school.

> They intended to be "ready for me" by "showing who's boss right away." To this paranoid kid it seemed that the Broughton administration was lying in wait for me. That became even clearer when I received an

advance copy of my fall class schedule. In spite of my answers to the "first, second, third choice" questions about classes, I was allocated a huge number of study halls that steered me away from courses in drama, art, history, etc. I was being assigned to supervised periods of boring silence. I had days scheduled with up to three study halls a day out of eight periods. They were ready for me, all right—ready to keep a close eye on me during most of the school day.

While these events were coming to a head, a reporter for the major Raleigh newspaper decided to tap into the parental views of it all. Interviewing Peggy, she asked, "How do you react to this publicity about your son?" In a reply quoted in the subsequent article, Peggy's answer reflected something of the educational philosophy implicit in this essay: "Fourteen-year-olds are beginning to try out various ideas and roles for themselves just as they try on various styles of clothing. We have to let them experiment, hoping that they do not damage themselves and others in the process." As late as 2005, a friend in Raleigh said to us: "I remember that comment of yours. It was right."

After 1969

Our son's life was irrevocably changed by that last year at Martin Junior High. For the next several years, he traveled the country on his thumb, went to work flipping hamburgers, became interested in theater, began to devour manuals on theater technology and engineering in general, founded a business as a self-taught electronic engineer, designed a sophisticated recording studio in New York City, and developed a reputation for building complex equipment down to the last exquisite detail. Never having attended a formal class in a university, he went on to prove that there are other forms of education for "getting ready for your future." He would always maintain that life itself was the great educator. In his self-education—exploring the country, reading the technical manuals, and conversations with many sorts of high achievers—his business began to prosper. By age twenty-seven, he had accompanied Harry Belafonte on a European tour, helped manage the sound system for Philip Glass's *Einstein On the Beach* in New York's Metropolitan Opera, handled the microphone feeds for an international press conference during the Dalai Lama's first visit to that city, and built a country house for his parents. Down the decades, he married, divorced, lost his business, and suffered accidents that left him partially disabled—and led to his death at age fifty-five in November 2009. He possessed a fabulous amount of knowledge about the world of electronic technology and the world in general. He often acknowledged sadly that American society denies lots of rewards to young people who disdain the rigors of high school, college, and graduate education. He himself would be the first to agree with the New York City schools chancellor's observation in 2009 that even "high school graduates can earn more than dropouts, have better health, more stable lives, and a longer life expectancy."

Like all summary biographies, this one does scant justice to the ups and downs of a life. If one were to identify one feature of the zigzag of his post-1969 ups and downs, it would be a stubbornness that pushed against every obstacle that the world pushed against him. Sometimes he won, sometimes he lost.

On the parental side of this mini-biography, his mother and I countered with our own stubbornness in our refusal to desert him while for years he appeared to desert us. That seeming desertion left his two parents struggling against waves of resentment, anger, and the temptation to answer desertion with desertion. This temptation was the stronger, given the excesses of behavior that afflicted thousands of young Americans in these years. Civil rights and war protest their parents could support; but when protest spilled over into drugs, alcohol, promiscuous sex, begging for a living, and carelessness about health, support easily turned into anger and grief. Must the adult world abandon all the ethics they try to teach their children when they offer them unconditional support for their public protests on behalf of certain elements in those ethics?

An element of the unconditional suffuses the parable of the Prodigal Son (Luke 15: 11–32). But only in some rarified sense can any human relation endure without some conditions. When the conditions are so comprehensively violated, parents begin to confront the temptations of abandonment. Parents who think themselves untouched by that temptation are either forgetful or blessed with the most cooperative of teenage children. They will not likely have had the experience of years' of unanswered letters, phone calls, and other forms of alienation, added to tokens of destructive behavior that contradict much in past and present parental example.

In the depths of despair and doubt over the effects of one's fallible efforts to be a parent, a struggle to care for one child can damage the effort to care for others. In one of the really touching conversations with our other children, ages twelve and eight in 1969, they said to us: "We sympathize with Greg, but we don't intend to be just like him. Remember, we are different." Paranoia in families is contagious. It can afflict parents, too. It can lead to an excessive attention to the black sheep to the neglect of the rest of the flock. Our other two children did not duplicate the feelings of the elder brother in the parable, but they did remind their parents that a justice which strains to care for a prodigal must not absorb all the energies that others in a family surely deserve.

Eventually, alienation was not to have its way with our eldest son. The precipitate of this experience has been the one sure bit of advice that we dare to offer other parents of other "challenging" children: *Hang in there.* They want you to be their parent even while they suggest otherwise. Decades later, they are likely to tell you so.

Though the overall challenges of 1968–69 for educators of my generation cannot be encapsulated in a single family experience, the longer I mediate on that year the more sobered I am by the interactive dynamics of families, institutions, peer groups, politics, and international affairs. The 1960s raised great questions about what is and is not the truest education of an upcoming generation of Americans. In these later years, Gregory became a partner in reflecting on the questions, and all of these pages owe much to our conversations. The experience recorded above raised many issues about education in the mind of this educator. Below are some of them.

What "family values" count most for a successful transition from childhood to adulthood?

In the summer of 1984, during my first visit to the Soviet Union, our Leningrad hosts offered us a mere hour to spend in one of the world's great art museums, the Hermitage. I had to decide what gallery to be sure to visit. I chose the Rembrandt. I knew that it housed the original of his "The Prodigal Son." When I got there, a crowd of Russian young people surrounded it, larger than any other gathering around any painting in the museum that day. I wondered if that painting struck some universal chord of pathos in the minds of these young people. It struck that chord in me.

From time to time in the journeys his mother and I have taken with Gregory, that parable and that painting have meant much to us. There are many forms of "prodigality" in families, and a child associated by a parent with that parable can feel insulted: who are parents to judge that I have "squandered my property in loose living" (Luke 15:13)? Parents can be prodigal, too. I have always wondered what fault might be charged against the father in the parable whose elder son fell prey to self-righteous disdain for the return of his brother. How on earth do two children in the same family turn out so differently? Few of us ordinary parents know how to answer that question, but from Jesus' story we ought to take encouragement from the phenomenon that, in spite all fallibility, parental love can persist. Religious professionals who work in urban ghettos of America often warn against telling young people there that "God's love is like a father's." Not so convincing an analogy, where fathers may be best known from having deserted mothers and children.

Not every middle class parent in America has experienced the temptation to stop being a parent to a wayward child. One speculates that in long-night, wakeful watches the father in the parable might have been similarly tempted. But the temptation did not win out for, when he saw that haggard son coming down the road, he ran to meet him. Neither did the temptation to forget about going home win in the mind of the Prodigal. Worth remembering is that the father was a rich man, a fact that calls to mind the fact that Americans are living through an era in which children may find it impossible to match the economic achievements of their parents' generation. Not only must they sometimes endure the shame of gross failure; they also have to cope with lowering their family's standards for success. They see parents as tough acts to follow. They are then the more inhibited from acting on the thought, in the midst of failure,

"My father's servants have more than enough bread. I will arise and go to my father" (Luke 15:18).

So, in the context of our family story here, I have to confess that there is one superordinate, educating "family value": love that refuses to let go, in spite of all. In modern American culture we tend to romanticize families, forgetting experiences of domestic hostilities that compelled the young priest in Bernanos's novel to say, "Families frighten me. We should say many prayers for them." Theology teaches me that human love is fragile, that only with great fear and trembling should any Christian blithely acclaim that "God's love is like a father's." That there is any clear analogy between that strong and this weak love borders on improbability, dishonesty, and trivial theology. Yet in human experience, there can be a love that persists in face of the temptations of abandonment. With the ruins of broken loves camping in and around most households, some of us can yet claim kinship with those hands of Rembrandt's father, resting there on the shoulders of that home-returning son.

One must not omit from celebration the fact that the son did eventually come home. Planting his feet on the road home was the necessary complement of the father's hands on his shoulders. No one can doubt the importance of such hands in the upbringing of young children, but the importance endures for humans of any age and on all sides of a fractured relationship. Surprising to me, at age eighty-two, has been the fact that one never really stops being a parent. Likewise, as Freud taught us, one never quite stops being a child. Children and parents access each others' hearts with a regularity that is sometimes painful. In that access, each has the beginning of something to lean on in the storms of history. I have to believe that even the flawed family can make this contribution to the long-range maturity of both children and parents.

Who and what are the educators?

The word "education" comes from a Latin word, "to lead out." The Socratic school would contend that the beginnings of wisdom are already there in the young mind, ready to be teased out. The biologists and sociologists of our time have a more interactive account: learning begins in a mother's womb whose liquid environment interacts with the world surrounding the mother. How else could anyone propose that Mozart is good for the newborn, maybe even the unborn?

The simple answer to the who and what of education has to be: Everything, everyone educates. In the boldness of his adult quest for glory, Tennyson's Ulysses might boast: "I am a part of all that I have met." But in fact the reverse was truer: All that he had met was a part of him. The ideology of American individualism to the contrary, we are shaped before we are shapers.

No one can be sure of the rank order of influences that shaped and misshaped the life of our son in that desperate 1968–69 year. That he absorbed political, ethical, and religious views from his family, we can be sure; but the pummeling of those views by forces as disparate as a junior high school, the Boy Scouts, the church, national and local news media, and peer group protesters made for a complex of "educators" that almost defies analysis. In the modern world there are no insulations between the personal, the familial, the local, the national, and the global contexts of education. This was the era when Marshall McLuhan was to tell us that our new electronic systems are vast extensions of our nerve ends. We now could view humans as they walked on the moon in the summer of 1969. Our telescopes were beginning to read old news from a Big Bang of 13.7 billion years ago.

But our new, infinite mazes of information can trouble finite human brains. Wordsworth found his nineteenth century world "too much with us." Our twenty-first century world can be too much for us by several orders of magnitude over his world. Cyberneticists speak blandly of the "information processing" of the human brain but also of "information overload." Overloads can threaten electrical circuits and human brains. They can persuade us to resort to terrible forms of personal defense, such as withdrawal into schizoid privacies that litter every ward of mental hospitals. There, conflicts in the mind can duplicate remote wars. Veterans of war carry their wounds decades into their future life. We now call those wounds "post-traumatic stress." So real and so persistent are those stresses that, for many Americans of the 1960s generation, the Vietnam War is not over. For many of its survivors, neither will the Iraq War be over soon.

Students of America in the 1960s like to describe the era as a time when the young rebelled against the old by defying institutions. Too little attention has been paid to the opposite analysis: how institutions rebelled against the young. Often missing from the lives of these young were adults who mastered the art of listening to the rage of the young without sharing all of it. The rage of protesters escalates when it falls on deaf or resistant ears of the older generation.

Another illustration from the 1968–69 biography of our eldest son fits here. As a longtime Boy Scout, like his father, he had fulfilled all the qualifications for scouting's highest rank of Eagle, except for a final interview with a committee comprised of representatives from the sponsoring church or other organization, plus adult troop leaders. In addition, in the wake of the Jesse Helms's editorials, two senior statewide scout leaders decided to attend this particular interview. The candidate's antiwar views soon came under scrutiny and his loyalty as an American. Toward the end of the discussion, the two visiting executives intervened with a recommendation that the Eagle Scout award be denied, "because he is not patriotic." Finally, to Gregory's aid came the third official member of the committee, his Presbyterian pastor. Pastoral influence won the day. Afterward the pastor, Albert Dimmock, testified to us two parents: "You would have been proud of how he answered those doubts about his patriotism. He maintained to his two critics that God was greater than country. That was what church and family had taught him. He pointed out to the critics that even the scouting award, 'God and Country,' which he had already earned, names 'God' before 'Country.'"

Later on, Gregory testified: "Maybe all those sermons I heard in the church and the conversations my father had with students considering conscientious objection, served me well after all."

Sad to remember, in the late 1960s adult defenders of the troubled young, especially in the American South, were too rare. Where at Martin Junior High were teachers and administrators who respected the consternation of bright male students at the prospect of being drawn into fighting a war that they deemed wrong and therefore unpatriotic? Where was an English teacher or two who honored fledgling eighth grade journalists with a critique of their angry prose so they could strengthen its appeal to other students, even state legislators? To have offered that sort of help would have run some risks for teachers. It was not easy in those days to express understanding of the revolt of the young against nationalism and education designed for shaping future employees of large corporations. Teachers can lose their jobs when they express too much understanding of precocious, troubled students.

More: teachers can lose their influence as teachers when they seem to love knowledge more than students. The role of affection, care, and companionship-in-learning is underappreciated by many educators. If they—we—paused more often to remember key moments in our own formal schooling, we might recover the insight that teachers must sometimes mediate between the rigors of official curriculum and the rigors of young rebellion. As noted in a previous essay, a Latin teacher in high school once offered me for study a literary essay by Cicero in place of the class's current boring-to-me Orations against Cataline. Like pastors, good teachers know that every human being is special. Among the burdens of modern high school teaching are the realities of large classes and looming Scholastic Aptitude Tests. Both can frustrate a teacher's hope of treating every student as special. The best side of the American penchant for individualism could be here. When the intellectual muscles of young begin to protest against "the establishment," why not draw them toward diligent inquiry into how establishments, traditions, and institutions can themselves fuel protest? Why not ask how institutions, by even old standards (like human rights and revolt in the name of religion), can be more humanely designed and administered?

At the end of my own college career in 1950, a dozen of us seniors got together to write recommendations for the improvement of the curriculum. On our side, it was an exercise of some *chutzpah*. But I shall never forget the comment of one professor upon reading our report: "Well, your education here could not have been a real failure if it stimulated you to come up with such a report."

Where were the teachers in that junior high who might have looked beneath the bad language and clumsy protest rhetoric in *Ignition* to discern young minds trying to cope with the impacts upon them of the modern world? Must public education be tethered to the rule, "Above all we aim to train the young to become loyal patriots"? Much in traditional American ideology breaks with that rule:

Jefferson, the abolitionists, and every proponent of the UN Declaration of Human Rights do so, as do most of the world's great religions. Young students who perceive the contradictions between conformist education and education-for-change are often the ones who ask the disturbing questions in many a classroom. Turning that disturbance into education is one challenge of real teaching. A recent film, *Freedom Writers*, based on an actual incident in Long Beach, California, vividly illustrates that challenge. Persisting in her attempt to bring education into an unruly high school classroom, a young teacher finally asks her students—many of them from broken families and communities—to write their life stories. Eventually, after three years together, teacher and students write and publish a book of those stories. The once impossible dream of college now became real for many of them.

How can families and schools prepare the young for their future response to the school of hard knocks?

Years after his launch into the post-school world of 1969, our eldest son said to us: "You taught us a lot about ethics and responsible human behavior. But you did not really prepare us for the meanness and the cruelties we were to encounter in school, work, business, and politics. Not everyone wishes me well."

The popular television detective series *Monk* begins with a song, "It's a jungle out there." The sergeant in another television series, *Hill Street Blues*, issues the same warning as colleagues are about to hit the streets. Given all the images of violence that pervade the media, video games, and history books, one might assume that no modern young person is ill-prepared to encounter violence in his or her lifelong surroundings. Cautious parents often try to protect their young against these images and realities. They discourage unregulated "televiewing," video fantasies of killing, and bloody movies. They do so knowing that the human world is probably not as pervasively violent as any night's TV dramas would suggest. They want a nonviolent domestic cocoon to provide children a counter to the jungle-image of the world. They hope that even violence-saturated drama will carry the message, "This is entertainment; it isn't real." I think of certain South African farm workers who, upon being invited by their employer to view the televised images of the falling World Trade towers on 9/11/01, said afterward, "We thought it was only a movie."

Competition, if not violence, is high on the agenda of most American educators. Many teachers see their task as preparing students to "compete in the world market." Not often mentioned in class are the troubling questions, "What happens to losers? How do you navigate failure? For self-respect, must you always be a winner? Must we not be open to new definitions of failure and success? How can we collaborate with new world partners?"

By growing up in the Vietnam era and leaving the cocoons of both family and formal education, our son early took on the harms of a competitive society as well as the opportunities. By starting at the bottom of the economic ladder and climbing higher on it than a less stubborn personality would have achieved, he became vulnerable to frustrations and exploitations that twenty-five-year-old graduates of business school may not have to cope with. In particular, as founder of his own business and employer of a dozen or so others, Gregory discovered that those others could not always be trusted to observe standards of justice, kindness, honesty, and promise-keeping. In one instance, assault and robbery almost destroyed him. In another, the failure of two marriages uncovered the dreaded potential of love to turn into hate. Finally and recently, violence entered and damaged his life in a car accident which challenged his lifelong stubborn will to let no obstacle threaten his survival.

Modern history and the daily news tell us that it is easy to destroy a life. Earthquakes and tsunamis raise the suspicion in us all that "nature" may be the enemy of our lives. So if we love life, we must guard it carefully. Only if we love it, however; otherwise, there is no "problem of evil" in the violence that can destroy us. Adolescents in urban ghettoes often say that they do not expect to live beyond age twenty-five because they live with daily drug-deaths and murder. In the Civil War, soldiers often wrote wills prior to a battle, taking courage and comfort from their certainty that someone back home really cared for them and would therefore read their letters. From one's own adolescence and that of our children and students, we know the question that rumbles in the depths of every developing self: "Am I lovable? Am I truly loved? Can I learn to love?"

At an early age, children do learn their mortality. If they are fortunate, in spite of death, they learn to answer "yes" to those pressing questions. They can learn it from many sources, the family first of all but also in institutions like schools and churches. Making that claim for schooling cuts across many a utilitarian argument for formal education. The information one acquires in a classroom one easily forgets, but not forgotten is the lesson that great teachers convey to some of their students: whatever your intellectual achievements or failures, your high grades or your low, whatever your compliance with our standards for predicting your present or future success, *you are worth teaching, for you are worth loving.* Tragedy in families, schools, and society at large comes whenever the young learn to doubt that. The most terrible personal result of racial prejudice in American society has been the thought in the minds of many African-Americans, "I really am inferior." No wonder a Jesse Jackson keeps on asking black people to shout, "I am somebody!"

Many times in those post-1969 years, the mother and father of our children had their claims to be Christians tested—almost beyond endurance. In those and subsequent years, we came often to experience the empirical as opposed to the idealistic realities of a religious commitment. We found ourselves reading the Bible often. We repaired to Luke 15 and to I Corinthians 13. From the latter, we became re-convinced from our experience as a family that "faith, hope, and love" really do "abide," neither without effort nor outside the tugs of daily life. The greatest of these three really is love: tough, battered, hurt, abiding love which persists against our shared human propensity for losing faith and hope in each other. Families may be frightening, but they are to be prayed for and struggled with. Our highest hope for them is that in them we can learn to love.

NOTES

1 Georges Bernanos, *The Diary of a Country Priest* (New York: Carroll and Graf, 1983), 188–89.

2 John Keegan, *A History of Warfare* (New York: Alfred A. Knopf, 1993), 50.

3 The rest of this essay is greatly indebted to Gregory, fifty-five years old in 2009 and living in Raleigh. In the summer of 2009, I submitted my first draft of this narrative to him, and he generously filled in certain facts and perspectives of which I may not have been aware. In various places, I have quoted his additions and duly noted that he supplied them. From a train of injuries and illnesses, he died on November 22, 2009.

Chapter 7

WHEN ECOLOGY BECOMES PERSONAL: TEN ACRES

௸

In tribute to Larry L. Rasmussen and Holmes Ralston III

"When the universe began the only elements were hydrogen and helium, leading one scientist to quip that gas, given enough time, turns into people."[1]

"Human existence is itself entwined with the primeval state of the universe."[2]

Five years after moving from Atlanta to New York City, I had gradually come to understand why so many New Yorkers have yearned to spend part of their year away from the city in a countryside close to "nature." The yearning has little to do with hatred of city life but rather with a sense that a world of concrete streets and tall buildings lacks a freedom and a joy that only an expanse of green things can supply.

The planners of the place called Manhattan, a century and a half ago, sensed this truth. The poet William Cullen Bryant helped them sense it. So they asked landscape architects Frederick Law Olmsted and Calvert Vaux to design a large plot of parkland in the center of the island. All 840 acres were to be reserved for rocks, trees, lakes, fields, squirrels, and human recreation. Between 1858 and 1876, a labor force of 3,000 and 400 horses moved a billion cubic feet of earth to sculpt those acres with imprints of the designers' humane vision of parkland.[3]

Many Manhattanites are sure that Central Park alone keeps NYC fit for human habitation. If one wants to entertain a politically impossible vision of a future NYC, try the idea of turning Central Park into real estate for business and apartment towers. Secularists who have lost touch with the idea of "sacred space" can be counted on to recover the idea if confronted with a serious proposal for turning Central Park into mere real estate. Their outrage would speedily become politics.

If one lives close to any of the island's parklands—Central, Riverside, Inman, Morningside, Union Square, and the Battery, for example—one has plenty of space for touching trees and plants like those which the original Munsee Indians left more or less undisturbed before the arrival of the Dutch and English. The latter landed on Manhattan with visions of world commerce in their brains. Like their capitalist successors, they did not hate the green things that blanketed the island on all sides of the thirteen mile Indian path that was to become Broadway. But they loved the big trees from an angle radically foreign to the minds of the Munsees and almost every other of the 500 Indian nations inhabiting this continent. For the enterprising European, trees could be *owned, bought, and sold.* As lumber for ship masts and houses, they were money.

Today the only trees in Manhattan, which were saplings when the Dutch—as myth has it—purchased the island for $24, are in Inman Park on the far northern tip of the island. Not mythical is the certainty that, whatever amount of money entered into the dealings between Europeans and the natives of this continent, few of the latter comprehended what the white man meant by "buying" a piece of land. Humans need land for their own survival, they knew; but they supposed that we live on land more as guests than owners. Like animals, we reserve territories for our own kin; but land for *sale*? Who would entertain such a presumption? The answer was: crazy Europeans.

Imbued with that craze, Americans old and modern long ago "conquered" the continent. Now it is ordinary investment wisdom that land is a very great source of wealth, so great that land ownership and land-value appreciation are basic to our powerful, unassailable cultural consensus as Americans. We make exception in cases like Central Park. No one knows the monetary value of those acres because no one is bold enough to put those acres on the market. Our earliest European ancestors entertained the idea of public land; but land for private possession, agriculture, status, and profit excited them most.

A certain extra-economic, land-centered dream does linger. City life to the contrary, we Americans have never lost our liking for wide-open spaces. We have built suburbs as places where we can eat the cake of income from a city center while having too the joy of green things. In my case, when I was thirteen, my parents built a house five miles from the office where my father worked as a lawyer in city government. The farmland suburb went up for sale when the longtime owner had to pay city taxes. Our quarter-acre lot lay close by a tidal river. It hosted a decaying oak tree 200 years old. By moving there, I came into close youthful association with the wonder of marsh wrens, gray herons, croakers, eels, blue crabs, and trees too large for human arms to reach around.

Then, in the suburban world of the wartime 1940s, with civilian construction virtually halted, you could use the remaining vacant neighborhood land for alleged support of the war effort. They called it "victory gardening."

Small children have intimate touch with dirt, but vacant suburban lots brought this adolescent into a more educating connection with dirt than childish mud pies had ever provided. Cut up a peck of potatoes, keep their "eyes" turned up, cover them with six inches of dirt, wait ninety days, and voila! There in the ground, thirteen pecks! It was enough to bring out the farmer in a city boy. It became one of my warmest memories: digging in that dirt with my father and watching vegetables grow.

That suburban mixture of city things and green things was the beginning of an education quite apart from the schools that have shaped much of my life. Only recently have I come to understand these entities—dirt, trees, gardens, and rivers—as educators of their human neighbors. Not until now, would I have named these things my educators. Ecologists have now taught me to listen consciously to this extra-human environment and to inquire, "What are these things saying to me?"

Scientists are our helpers in translating the languages of dirt into terms humans can understand. I have to take their word for these things, as do Holmes Rolston, Annie Dillard and Larry Rasmussen. They quote biologists as finding,

> ". . . in one square foot of topsoil one piddling foot deep 'an average of 1,356 living creatures, including 865 mites, 265 springtails, 22 millipeds, 19 adult beetles, and various numbers of 12 other forms.' (And that doesn't include two billion bacteria and millions of fungi, algae, and innumerable other creatures that make the topsoil the one inch of *adama* it is."[4]

> "There is in a handful of humus, which may have ten billion organisms in it, a richness of structure, a volume of information (trillion of 'bits'), resulting from evolutionary processes across a billion years of history, greatly advanced over anything in myriads of galaxies, or even, so far as we know, in all of them."[5]

My advanced education in these matters owes much to contemporary scholars like the above three. Add to them the names Loren Eiseley and Lewis Thomas. In addition, for the past thirty years, Peggy and I have engaged in "field work" on the subject in summertime residence on a parcel of rural land a hundred miles north of New York City. The following is a sketch of what that plot of a little less than ten acres has been teaching me.

Ten Acres

If you are a Manhattanite, why arrange a rural retreat for one's self and family when you can wander in Riverside and Central Park to your heart's content? The answer is: if you dare to live for months surrounded by woods growing on a former sheep farm, your attention to green things gets daily, exquisitely *concentrated*. You ask of that hillside what you cannot ask of a city park: the right to dig in it and the right to build a house on it. More profoundly, you now are engaged in a dialogue with land whether you meant to have conversation with it or not. Illusory as our notion of ownership may be, to say that those acres "belong" to you invites the experience of discovering how you belong to it.

The ownership of a country retreat also brings an acknowledgment that you belong to a city, too. Americans who purchase a second home in the country soon have to admit that they do not really envy those Indians and Europeans who undertook errands into a real wilderness. The modern city follows us into the country in a hundred forms which few of us are willing to abandon: electricity, telephones, television, computers, and the multitude of technical services that skilled townspeople will provide their hillside neighbors on call. Country life in modern America is a compromise between metropolis and meadow. Only the bravest of the brave among us spend even one month in a true wilderness. Often in our thirty years in Columbia County, I have thought gratefully of a New Deal government in the 1930s that invented the Rural Electrification Administration. Electricity introduced a new degree of equality in the connections of urban and rural Americans. Most of all, it put the most isolated prairie farmers in touch with the world and the world in touch with them. Indeed, thanks to technological connections, the radical split between local and global has now almost vanished. In the multitude of our human-made, worldwide connections, we have been readied for learning the great overarching truth that the ecologists now are teaching us: every thing is connected with every thing. No time, no space exists alone. It is all interrelated. It's called a universe.

The connections are vast, incalculable, and all-present. To be sure of this, we can start either at the remote beginnings of the Big Bang or in the smallest corner of a garden. In the summertime, on our ten acres, I pay a morning pastoral call on our garden. I keep the sprouting vegetable seeds watered. I nourish the flowers with mulch. Not long ago. I had raised from seed a few zinnias. Transplanting one of them, I pressed dirt down around its roots and reflected that maybe in so doing I was obeying the ancient instruction that we humans are to "till and keep" the earth (Genesis 1:28). Here I was, good steward of a green thing, keeping that zinnia, encouraging it soon to bloom. It felt good: I was doing my duty to a zinnia. I was taking care of it.

But then data from the astronomers and biologists punctured my paternal feeling for that zinnia. The man was taking care of the plant, but the plant was also taking care of the man. With the million green leaves of my immediate horizon, the zinnia was breathing out the oxygen that I was breathing in twenty times a minute. The earth sciences tell us all about this benign interchange. Although living from that interchange, our ancient human ancestors may not have known how dependent they were on green things. But now we do know. While breathing out oxygen, leaves breathe in carbon dioxide from our lungs. We are a symbiosis. If we were ever to come to a survival contest between us organics and that world of plants, they would win. They can probably get along without us oxygen-breathers; we could not get along without them. As of 2009, mournfully enough, the biologists warn us that earth's greenery is having its capacity tested for absorbing our other, industrially-generated carbon dioxide. Those leaves cannot absorb an infinite amount of that compound. The excess is going into atmospheric warming.

But there is another compound as immediate to my survival in that rural setting. It's as invisible as the oxygen. We get to it by digging into dirt and rock. We could get along for a few days without electricity, but not without that great combination of hydrogen and oxygen: *water*!

No wise home builder on a rural hillside had better start building before determining if there is water flowing underneath that ground. Deep-digging drills can access this blessed liquid down several hundred feet of clay and stone. As our luck would have it, our ten acres lay atop one of the region's great underground waterways: the Berkshire aquifer. We get rudely informed about our dependence on that invisible river every time thunderstorms and vulnerable electric lines connive to disable our electric pump 273 feet below. Humans cannot live ten minutes without oxygen. It is not easy to live ten hours without water. When the blizzards of winter come, the cutoff of electrical service can be more frequent. Then, the urban migrant may entertain the ironic thought, "Better to return for a while to the big city? It seems to have a steadier electric grid." Ah so? When that urban grid goes out, millions are in the dark; in the countryside, only thousands. Well that we can still breathe in the dark. In city or country, we live from water, too.

The more inclusive truth is that industrialism and nature surround us in such intimate connection that "back to nature" is only a dream for most of us. During his youth in Virginia, Holmes Ralston III had to walk from town into mountains to get in touch with real wilderness. He settled in Colorado partly to be in touch with a western American wilderness that is vaster than we Easterners are likely to know.

The very word "wilderness" carries threatening overtones in the ears of most of us. John the Baptist survived there on locusts and wild honey, and Jesus retreated there for a forty day fast. Few of us moderns relish the thought of hunger for forty days, even for the most spiritual of reasons. Indeed, almost all the people of the Bible lived in the "second revolution" of human civilization: agriculture. Even the first chapters of Genesis assume that humans have become earth-tillers, no longer hunters and gatherers in forests and plains. For their participation in the sacrament of baptism, Christians should remember how the River Jordan made some of that wilderness livable. Every time we participate in the Eucharist, we touch the fact that Jesus chose two products of the agricultural revolution to connect members of the beloved community to its Creator.

Cultural Tags in Our Eyes for "Nature"

Occasionally an item in our flower garden touches me with a different kind of love. One is the spider lily which blooms annually just outside our front door. For its short season, its six yellow petals tremble in the wind one day, then next day droop in death as do all day lilies. This year its buds numbered forty. I loved every one of them and mourned the shriveling of the last. It is easy to concentrate on that graceful flower in a moment shorn of historical association. Doubtless lilies have a history locked away in fossils of some geological stratum. For the moment, I enjoy those blossoms as history's gift to me on a summer morning. I do not need to know its ancient origins.

But certain other features of our hillside are not so easily separated from associations that a modern plant lover brings to his or her view of flowers. On the day of that lily's debut, I chanced upon two other gifts of the woods. One was the berries on a beechnut tree. My generation of American children has an absurd association with beechnut: the name of a chewing gum. We could imagine those berries from the wrapper long before we ever saw a real beechnut tree. That association is innocent enough. But within my half hour's walk came into view another flower with a radically less innocent association that could only be imposed on it by a human of my generation.

It was a single wild rose, peeping out from under a carpet of periwinkle. A circle of stamens surrounded its pistil center against a backdrop of five pink petals. Swiftly I thought of the music of Edward McDowell, and then of the European Union whose flag of circular stars resembles that circle of stamens. Finally something more ominous stared at me in that rose. Its five petals formed a nearly perfect pentagon. There may have been a day when "pentagon" merely recalled to high school students their class in plain geometry. Not so for us of the twentieth century. For us, it recalls a building in Virginia that houses the headquarters of the largest military organization in human history and that suffered broken walls and broken people in an attack of terrorists on 9/11/01.

What a burden to project onto one little flower! What a heavy history to bring to one's view of it, and how immediately this viewer wishes that he could deliver his pleasure at the sight of that wild flower from the grim drapery of modern world history. Technologies of countryside and city do infiltrate each other. Our minds can mingle a vast set of global facts with our enjoyment of even the sunniest day in the country. On such a day, September 11, 2001, our country view of collapsing buildings in our city and the ripped side of our Pentagon came via television. People on the scene will always remark on what a lovely, clear, sun-bright September day it was, an ideal day for a late summer stroll at the beach, in the park, or on a hillside. For most of us modern Americans, seldom has a bright day in nature collided with such a dark day in human history, and seldom have citizens of the world had so stark a reason to think that the natural world and the human world are a dualism, two realities made separate by human tragedy and evildoing. Gravity did its ordinary work bringing down those tall towers and killing those 2,970 human beings. But the real killers were other human beings.

Recent public debate in the United States has swirled around the question: Does the universe show signs of a divine Designer? Is there intelligence and benign purpose evident in the long history that began with a Big Bang? Most of us who believe in the Creator of it all are inclined to answer "of course!" But we are also inclined to sidestep the theological debate by asking if human beings themselves evidence intelligence and purpose in their ragged history. Aside from the strange interconnections of stardust, planets, and organic earthen life, do we humans demonstrate any *kindly* intelligence inborn in ourselves? I stand with that young visitor to Egypt who, on a starry night beside the Sphinx, asked his companion, "If you could ask the Sphinx one question, what would it be?" Replied the other, "I think I would ask, 'Is the universe friendly?'" But my choice of question would be the more troubling: "Are we human beings friendly, friendly enough to stop killing each other?"

Among a rare subset of philosophers who dare to ask these questions, none has been more honest and searching that Holmes Rolston III. Philosophers and theologians long ago managed to divide the "problem of evil" into two categories: natural and moral. The separation is hard to maintain, for what looks like evil in nature to our human eyes may simply be what is bad for us or damaging to something we value. We are too anthropocentric in our definitions of evil. We may even be too centered on "life" in contrast to all the natural forces that both sustain life and sustain each other apart from life. It is hard for us, however, not to value the life of earth's animals and trees above the existence, say, of a nova about to explode. If earthly life—all creatures great and small—is valuable, if something special is going on in the long evolution of the gases toward earth creatures, if earth is host to creatures that we must value more highly than we value mere atoms and molecules, our definitions of "the problem of evil" must finally center on the array of forces that support or damage life.

Rolston has pioneered ecological ethics in his stout assertion of values inherent in the evolution of various earth species. The eagle that soars above the tree line is a thing of beauty as well as a bird of prey. Even in preying on certain other creatures, the eagle serves the survival of other forest creatures and they the eagle. When we humans assert that eagle flight is beautiful, we project something from our own minds; but why deny that eagles, dolphins, and even day lilies incorporate in themselves some inner regard for their graces, skills, and attractions to other beings in their own?

I was taught in literature classes that such thinking verges on "the pathetic fallacy," projecting onto the natural world feelings and subjectivity knowable only in the human world. Nonetheless, setting aside for a moment the problem of moral evil in human history, the lover of life in the natural world has a problem, too. The forces of death are strong in that world. Serenity in face of that fact can easily be achieved through the observation that in nature death serves intergenerational life. If old life never died, new life might never live. So what's the problem?

The problem got posed years ago by C. E. M. Joad in his book, *God and Evil*. On speaker's corner in London's Hyde Park, a Christian evangelical praised the workings of divine purposes in the world. Again and again, as the testimony continued, a heckler in the crowd shouted, "What about fish cancer?"

My local version of that protest might be, "What about gypsy moths?" The first year of our residence on our country hillside was the year that the moths visited the Northeast. Their local predations centered on our 90-year-old white oak. We knew its age because, when we had to cut it down, we counted the rings in the trunk. Over the summer season, as the moths finally departed, leaving the oak haggard, we saw demonstrated the classic struggle of a species to survive the onslaughts of its enemies. Our oak grew a new midsummer coat of leaves, which we admired while hoping for its resurrection from near-death. To no avail; by next spring, our magnificent oak qualified for firewood. As we counted its rings, I calculated that its seedling had sprouted from an acorn just ten years before the birth of my father in 1901.

Must we humans look with serenity at the competition of species in the world of green and organic things? Am I justified in hoping for a long life of oaks as well as a long life for ourselves? If humans are now among the great historic enemies of millions of earth creatures, are we then only imitators of those creatures themselves? What nerve we have for preferring the prosperity of oak trees over the prosperity of leaf-hungry moths! Let Darwin and his disciple Thomas Huxley speak for us all: Life is a contest between lives, the "fittest" must survive, and the sometime human propensity for helping the evolutionary losers is profoundly misguided.

I confess to a growing willingness to be so misguided. A few years after the destruction by moths of that magnificent white oak, the electric company sent its workers up our long driveway with instructions to clear the wires of trees whose branches could damage the wires during storms. They worked outside our ten acres and proceeded to cut down not an oak but a maple of similar great age. Afterwards, I wrote a letter to the president of the power company. I said, "You know, a tree that has survived lightning and other threats for eighty or ninety years deserves some respect for its achievement, don't you think? Your wires had to cross from one side of the road to the other, but why not beat a detour around that great maple tree?" To his credit, the president replied saying, "Perhaps you are right. We might be more careful next time." It was a refreshing contrast to the excuses he might have offered such as, "You can't have power lines without destroying some trees. Do you want electricity or not?" That sort of technological determinism accounts for vast destructions of forests across the planet. In the Amazon basin, it's people or trees.

In recent years, I have had my instinct of respect for aged trees expanded into a much wider respect for the whole of sentient life around me. Three of my teachers have been Eiseley, Ralston, and Rasmussen. Eiseley was a professional paleo-anthropologist turned philosopher and poet. His intellectual opening to ethics and religion attracted little honor from his University of Pennsylvania colleagues and others in the scientific community. He carefully studied the findings of Darwin. He often pondered the mixture of care and carelessness in relations between species. One day, as he wondered in the woods, he came across a lethal battle between a black snake and a pheasant. Coiled around the bird, the snake apparently was ready to kill her in his attempt to possess the eggs in her nest. Eiseley decided to step in and separate the snake from the bird. Afterward he wondered if was right to do so. Ought soft-hearted humans to resist their instinct for protecting the survival of one species over another? Ought we to confess to the hypocrisy of our dislike of competition between species in nature while tolerating our destruction of various species if our needs require it? Who says that some species, having so far won the evolutionary competition, must be preserved ad infinitum? "A thousand types are gone," mourned Tennyson in *In Memoriam* as he wrestled with ideas of evolution already in the air prior to Darwin's *The Origin of Species*. Huxley's transfer of the survival contest in nature to human competition was soon to flow "naturally," one might say, into new versions of racism in nineteenth century images of humans. Nature sets the pattern: look out for your own kind. Look out for the best subset of your kind: for example, your white skin over their dark skin. The best adapted become the strongest, and the strongest have a right to dominate and destroy the weakest. It's a "law" of nature.

Eiseley's contradiction of this version of evolution rested on an urge in him, not in the rest of nature. He believed that it was right for humans to dream of a "reconciliation" of all creatures to each other's existence. He does not quote it, but he could have resorted to the ancient biblical vision of "the peaceable kingdom" (See Isaiah 11:6–8). Humans have hopes for the world not found in any other creature. Not every death-dealing contest among the creatures are we called to imitate. But we are responsible, Eiseley believed, to include *ourselves* in our accounts of the "natural." Snakes may not be ours to kill, but when they are about to kill the next generation of some pheasants, perhaps our own intuitions should come into active play.

Another latter-day refutation of the Huxley-Spencer version of evolutionary ethics came recently from the late Lewis Thomas. Nature has a way, he said, of assisting the survival of species by the formation of partnerships. The carbon dioxide-oxygen partnership between trees and organic life is one illustration among thousands. Bees and flowers survive together, thistle seeds and goldfinches, monarch butterflies and milkweed, pilot fish and sharks, the lioness and her cubs, and human neighbors who protect each other in the path of hurricanes.

But that refutation went only partway. There was Lewis Thomas, pitting his professional energies against the ravages of cancer in human beings, finally succumbing to that disease himself. Might a commodious ethic have permitted him to shift his scientific energy and intelligence from humans to fish? Might his answer to the Hyde Park heckler have been, "We must use our human intelligence to combat fish cancer, too." That retort would comport with a famous early twentieth century essay by William James, "The Moral Equivalent of War." There he urged us to turn our aggressive energies towards nature, to build dikes against floods, tree breaks against erosion, and places for creatures to hide from tornadoes. James' analogy to warfare seemed to fit the spirit of the early twentieth century, heir to Huxley's sermons, on the cusp of a great world war. But the metaphor was a bad auspice for the ecological vision that Rachel Carson would initiate fifty years later. Making "war" on nature for human purposes defies the great ecological fact: we are all on this earth together in a vast mutual interdependence. War on nature entails war on ourselves. Start destroying the nature we do not like, and we may have begun to destroy *Homo sapiens*, too. As Eiseley liked to warn, our very concept of a "nature" apart from ourselves prepares our minds for facile nature devastation. He quotes Pascal: "There is nothing which we cannot make natural," and "there is nothing natural which we do not destroy."[8]

The new ecology yields much reason to believe that we all live more by partnerships than by contests. Even so, the problem of evil in nature does not disappear. Cancer in fish, gypsy moths in oaks, and all those forces on earth antagonistic to the life of this and that species, ought to continue to worry us. Among the partnerships most worrisome to us and our human neighbors in Columbia County, New York, is that between field mice, deer, and the tiny tick that carries Lyme disease. The statistics so far identify our county as the world's epicenter of the disease. If worry about fish cancer is appropriate to humans, worry about Lyme is appropriate, too.

The great issue is how we are to understand the scope of our responsibilities inside the webs of our eco-human lives. Scientists may want to avoid the question. Exits from such concern they are likely to see as native to science itself.

To counter the easy exits, Holmes Rolston, like Eiseley

and Rasmussen, has devoted many years to observing natural environments and thinking about the human place in those environments. He accepts the account of astrophysicists concerning how the foundations for organic life were laid in the earliest moments of universal history. In those moments, thirteen and one half billion years ago, helium turned into hydrogen and soon after oxygen emerged along with iron and carbon. The universe was set on a journey towards life. Rolston's masterful conclusion is that the universe honors life, evolves and protects life in "upswing" after upswing.

> [N]ature, inclusive of natural selection, is a story-spinning system. It no doubt selects for survival, but its arrivals tell ongoing stories, those of contributions, conflicts, and crises in a "storied fight" from matter to life, life to mind, mind to culture, and culture to spirit, a fight through good and evil.[9]

As both an honest observer of earthen life and a philosopher-theologian, Ralston knows that the paths to life on this singular earth-planet have not been smooth or uncluttered with vast destruction. Anti-life evolves with life, and for every upswing there is often a hidden downswing.

Rolston himself is troubled by those downswings, but he resists too prompt a human judgment on good and evil in natural systems, based on our own value preferences. We know enough about biology, for example, to wonder why rogue cancer-inducing body cells became a part of this world in the first place. Why the hospitality of the anopheles mosquito to a malaria virus? Why that virus? Most of us have been asking these age-old questions since at least our adolescence. Early on, we learned to quarrel with alleged answers from the philosophers and theologians, but I have to confess that a bit of adolescent spirit survives in my mature musing over the questions. Nothing in Aristotle's concept of "final cause" lifts our burden here, and not even the Apostle Paul settles the matter for Christians in his triumphant faith that "in everything God works for good with those who love him, who are called according to his purpose" (Romans 8:28). I remain skeptical that there is anything good coming out of fish cancer or our own.

Perhaps skepticism is too arrogant a human response to these impenetrable questions. Rolston combines "upswings in favor of life" in this corner of the universe with admiration for the unique powers of the human brain and a certain strain of agnostic humility. Who are we to be sure that mosquitoes are unnecessary for the evolution of this ecosystem? Will we discover too late the cost to ourselves and the earth of our destruction of thousands of species? If we destroy the Amazon forest, what drugs will we lose that have served the survival of other species and that might yet serve our own?

Beyond the wisdom of such agnostic confession, however, there remains another problem: The problem of the good! Why should it exist? Old theologies, counter to a biblical faith in one Creator of one universe, assigned evil to a dualism, even to another creator. Not so the orthodox of the centuries: biblical faith supports the belief of most scientists that we inhabit a universe, one realm of reality. For neither humans nor for other creatures does everything work for good. But some things do work for good, a fact that should inhibit all radical super-moral skepticism, such as Ivan Karamazov famously asserted. With the easy exit of dualism closed, we cannot avoid Voltaire's withering satire of Candide. But we will not doubt the undeniable presences of both great good and great evil in our experience of the world.

As moralists have long known, the problem of natural evil is almost insurmountable for our reasoning powers. Who can join Candide in declaring Lyme and malaria parts of the best of all possible worlds? The best response we can muster is apparently an imitation of William James—mobilize our powers to protect ourselves and our fellow creatures from senseless destruction. We will not identify evil with death, however, or with suffering; but we will hold on to the difference—with the ancient Hebrews—between death-in-maturity and death-too-soon. We will continue to believe that wisdom can come from some suffering over against the suffering that has no wisdom and no use in it. Abraham Heschel, Rasmussen, and Eiseley are attuned to the unique phenomenon in humanity of empathy and love that suffers with the suffering of the other. Rolston quotes the longtime student of chimpanzees, Jane Goodall, as conceding that they "usually show a lack of consideration for each other's feelings which in some ways may represent the deepest part of the gulf between them and us." A gulf that we humans have yet to cross in depth and with consistency! Our human, embodied mind, observes Rolston, "is not hardware, not software, it is (so to speak) wetware that must be kept wet, sometimes with tears, struggling to do right, surrounded by wrongs."[10]

Wisest of all early biblical insights here might be the Genesis warning that we are not the final possessors of the "knowledge of good and evil." We do not know good and evil as the Creator knows them, and it is arrogant to be "too sure that we are right" in these matters.[11] Maybe the gypsy moths have a place in the long distance journey of our habitat? We are wise to keep the question while also holding to our judgment that fish and oaks and human children are worth saving from their enemies. Those enemies, ironically, include humans themselves.

That brings me back to our ten acres.

The World and All in It as Gift and Finite Human Task

Among his eloquent appropriations of scientific knowledge of how everything we know is connected to many things we do not know, Larry Rasmussen quotes Alice Walker's character Shug, who abandons a belief in the "old white man's God" but acquires new belief in the moment when she felt that she was "a part of everything." She now sees herself as part of an astonishing world that cannot be wholly understood by humans but that must be admired.

> "Listen, God love everything you love—
> and a mess of stuff you don't. But more than
> anything else, God love admiration."In
> particular, God loves trees, because "trees
> mean life that has staying power."[12, 13]

For me that assault on an old Maple by the power company insulted its staying power, so also the gypsy moths on our oak. Fair protest, I have to conclude, against both human and insect invasions. Such protest leaves an unsettled logic in its wake: ecosystems deserve human respect, but is all of it respectable? The contradiction will not go away. One way to make it go away is to accept the compromise which Voltaire urges on Candide: one must cultivate one's own garden. But that is isolationist advice in conflict with admiration, respect, and care for an environment quite outside our garden. Indeed, in my own early attempts at gardening on our hillside, we were consistently defeated by the hunger of our deer, our raccoons, and our groundhogs. Asserting our right to raise lettuce and tomatoes, we built fences, reasoning that one-fifth of our ten acres should rightly be a preserve for our uses while we left the four-fifths to our creaturely neighbors. For a while, we trapped the raccoons—twenty-eight of them over several years—and carted them off to a wild space recommended by the local game warden. Then the plague of rabies invaded the region's raccoons, removing much of that problem from gardeners while leaving us to cope always with deer. It is neither consistent nor eco-ethical of us, however, to take smug satisfaction in the way nature is curtailing the raccoon population. What right have we to protest those gypsy moths while happily accepting that rabies? I shall never forget seeing one diseased raccoon limping across the road on its way to dying. I wanted to say to him: "Creature-neighbor, I hate to see you suffer, yet I hate too your habit of eating our vegetables. Was there not enough healthy greenery for you and the deer to eat on acres outside our fences? And, by any chance, is the agricultural research lab at Cornell University working on rabies in your species, or are they just trying to protect us from your diseases?"

I am comforted in all of this neither by Voltaire's isolationist advice nor by Emerson's assertion that "a foolish consistency is the hobgoblin of little minds." Consistency in promoting one's own human interests against the interest of trees and hungry animals may not qualify as foolish, but it certainly does qualify as a difficult, troubling challenge. "Let each kind look out for itself" is a tempting practical solution to this conflict, but it is not so practical now that our self-interest in destroying other earth species turns out to be self-destructive. Neither is this worrisome conflict resolvable by the history of nature's own abolition of species. Inside our "gardens," we hunker down in the anthropocentric hope that the destructive effects of volcanoes, tornadoes, and diverse diseases can be confined to creatures other than ourselves.

Perhaps the loudest lesson gleamed from these thirty years of listening to our ten acres, then, is their call for humility in us, their guests on this hillside. As if patience with the weather were not enough for encouraging this virtue, we know we have to fit our preferences into this woody hillside with the preferences of many other creatures. As the ecologists urge us, we want to understand the roles of each in the workings of the whole hillside ecology. We even hope that the scientists will tutor us in the ecological uses of all 1,356 bugs in that one square foot of topsoil. As our admiration for bugs expands, we may be excused for opposing the imperial passion of some for eating our lettuce and tomatoes.

Humans like to know the "why" of everything. But in an advanced, thirty year wrestle with these ten acres, I am left with more mystery than satisfied theory and practice. For the perceptive eye, earth *is* "crammed with heaven, and every bush *is* aflame with God."[13] We will never be satisfied to join those who merely "sit round and pick blackberries" at behest of human taste and needs. Perhaps, before we start eating blackberries, we ought to admire them as beautiful, nutritious creatures, as our companions with all the sustaining oxygen, nitrogen, and rotted leaves which the Big Bang bequeathed to us. So many gifts we benefit from, long before we acknowledge or understand them!

Not long before he died at the end of a Nazi hangman's noose, Dietrich Bonhoeffer wrote:

> Without gratitude my past sinks into
> darkness, mystery, nothingness. And yet,
> in order not to lose my past, which God has
> given me, but to regain it, gratitude must
> be complemented by contrition. In gratitude
> and contrition my present life and my past
> are united.[14]

No modern human, from even a little knowledge of recent earth-history, should lack for reasons to be contrite about how our species has damaged this eco-sphere. But in the order of eco-ethical priority, gratitude comes first, contrition next, and gratitude again. Earth is the world in which "we live and move and have our being." In that quotation from

On Second Thought

a Greek philosopher, the Apostle Paul tried to describe our relation to our Creator to a sophisticated Athens audience (Acts 17:28). Our new ecological knowledge invites us to acknowledge that the Creator touches us at all points and moments of the creation. God is present to us in everything and in every time. Ancient Hebrews heard divine law in a divine revelation to their ancestors, but one late deliverance of that law reminded them that the word of God was now "very near you; it is in your mouth and in your heart that you can do it" (Deuteronomy 30:12). That assurance needs broad reinterpretation in the coming era of "earth ethics and earth community." In the midst of that new earth-wide ethic, we who see in our "natural" surroundings an abundance of divine gifts must be prompted by those gifts to celebrate the survival of many others not of our kind. We cannot rationally explain how or why this creation should be a habitat for elephants, earthworms, oaks, and humans together. But we can be sure that we do belong together, that we are mutually connected, that we need each other, and that we should learn to serve each other's survival. We the human partners in it all are mystified and distressed at the diseases and plagues that destroy ourselves and our neighbors. We humans, at least, are called to work to cure diseases as we can, to hold back some of the floods, and to protect some of the birds from the predations of snakes. But like our powers, our ethics and our glimpses of the divine are finite. We cannot be grateful for all the mysterious destructive conflicts in our environment. Like Job, we need reminding that our eyes, ears, and brainpower are not up to grasping the "reason" in it all. Like true science, our true response to a mysterious universe and to the mysteries of life on our precious planetary home has to be a compound of wonder, gratitude, and contrite repentance for our arrogance. The gifts of our Creator summon us to works of love.

One irreducible experience of our summertime life on our ten acres has been wonder. Cities are places so organized by human concerns that standing stupefied under a starry night sky is not a daily occurrence for most urbanites. Not so for us during the summer on our hillside. There on some cloudless evenings, a Milky Way–bright night sky glimmers. The astronomers and cosmologists have told us that we are looking at the "milk" of clusters of stars numbering in the billions. A light beam, they say, takes 100,000 light-years to cross this local galaxy.

I think often of Psalm 139 in those moments under stars. If this starry sky does not reduce one to wonder, what will? And how in the midst of bafflement at it all, can we earthlings not be grateful for wonder itself, our human ability to wonder "where we are (cosmology, universe, Earth, creation), who we are (person, self, spirit, soul, made in the image of God), what we ought to do (ethics, justice, love, value choices)."[15] Being human is a large order, a long adventure, and a great privilege. Our world is a glorious place. We are part of its glory.

NOTES

1 Larry Rasmussen, *Earth Community, Earth Ethics* (Maryknoll, NY: Orbis Books, 1996), note 35, 262.

2 Holmes Rolston III, *Science and Religion: A Critical Survey* (New York: Random House, 1987), 69, quoting astronomer Bernard Lovell.

3 Washington Irving and George Bancroft took up Bryant's dream, terming the proposed location "waste land, ugly and repulsive," because inhabited by squatters in shanties and criminals. In the Great Depression of the 1930s, the squatters returned, making a "Hooverville." See *The Michelin Guide to New York City* (Lake Success, NY: Michelin, 1975), 101.

4 Ibid., 263. The name Adam in Genesis derives from the Hebrew word for earth or topsoil and the name Eve from the Hebrew for "living." Together, notes Rasmussen, "Adam and Eve signify 'Soil and Life.'"

5 Holmes Rolston III, *Three Big Bangs: Matter/Energy, Life, Mind* (New York: Columbia University Press, Forthcoming 2010), chapter 2. Used by permission.

6 Agriculture, industrialism, and information are tags of three "revolutions" in the last 5,000 years of human history. Rolston puts these changes in a vaster cosmic perspective when he distinguishes three stages of universal history in three "Big Bangs": the physical, the biological, and the informational or cybernetic. He sees the human brain as the climax of this history, which is not duplicated in any star system known to us.

7 See Loren Eiseley, *The Firmament of Time* (New York: Atheneum Books, 1966), 173–8l.

8 Ibid., 159.

9 Rolston III, *Science and Religion*, 275.

10 Rolston III, *Three Big Bangs*, chapter 3. Quotes from Jane Goodall in van Lawick-Goodall, 1971, 194.

11 This was Justice Learned Hand's definition of "the spirit of liberty," which would seem to apply to scientific and religious humility as well.

12 Rasmussen, *Earth Community, Earth Ethics*, 203–204, quoting from Alice Walker, *The Color Purple* (New York: Pocket Books, 1982), 178.

13 Elizabeth Barrett Browning, in her verse novel, *Aurora Lee*. Emphasis mine.

14 Dietrich Bonhoeffer, "Fragments from Tegel," The Collected Works of Deitrich Bonhoeffer, Volume 16, *Konspiration und Haft* (Guetersloh: Christian Kaiser Verlag, 1996), 492.

15 Rolston III, *Three Big Bangs*, chapter 3.

Chapter 8

Serving the Future by Unsettling the Present: Leadership

❧

"The longer one works at being president, the more visible to him or her become the impacts of the present upon the future. Educating any generation of humans to the welfare of future generations will never be easy. The ecology movement teaches this truth in painful abundance; I learned it definitively at Union Seminary."[1]

About a year before I received, out of the blue, an invitation to become the thirteenth president of Union Theological Seminary in New York, I was having lunch with my wife Peggy. Once again we were running over the questions that a forty-six-year-old seems to ask as his professional career is at least half over: "Is this what I ought to be doing? Has it added up to anything important so far?" With the wisdom and humor that I have come to expect of her, she looked me in the eye and said, "I think it is about time that we declared your life a success."

It was not only the right word but the important word a year later as we were considering the biggest job I had ever been offered. The job had in it some huge challenges and a measure of prestige. In thinking about this prospect, I had to tell myself, *I do not need this job to affirm my worth or my identity.*

We Protestants value the idea of "calling," an urgency about the path down which God may be calling one to go. I have learned to resist the idea that God has only one path into the future, or only one way of assuring us human beings that we count for something. Alas: in contrast to the basic Protestant doctrine that we are "saved by faith, not by works," we nonetheless like the assurances of good works. We even prefer to have that assurance in advance! From the culture of the black church I have learned to think differently about vocations. A "call" is an invitation to a journey. To accept the call is to join the black spiritual, "I'm gonna lay my burdens on the Lord, and I will go, I shall go to see what the end will be."

My call to Union was thirty-four years ago. I am glad now that I accepted it in the freedom not to accept it, and the freedom to quit the job at any time. As it happened, I kept the job for sixteen years. Below is an analysis of certain challenges in those years, and some theological-ethical dimensions in those challenges which kept me "keeping on keeping on."

Problems and Tensions that Presidents are Likely to Face

I have long admired Sir Geoffrey Vickers's writings about the policies he and others devised as members of the British civil service, especially his concept of the "multi-valued choice." Ethicists have some natural affinities for the reality that most of the difficult choices in human affairs lie not between competing good and evil but between competing goods. Below I identify some major problems that camped about my office during my sixteen years there. In these tensions between competing goods, others may find themselves able to identify the commonalities that bind all presidents in all institutions into one great fellowship of shared perplexity.

Personal History and Appropriation of Organizational History

In one of the wry comments for which he was famous, Professor C. Ellis Nelson once remarked, "At Union nothing has a reason; everything has a history." He was putting his finger on the conservatism of an organization that publicly prides itself on being the home of liberals, radicals, and cutting edge innovators. Living up to history is a challenge for the constituents of every institution, including those whose leaders want to use history for change.

Aware that I was an outsider to the history of Union (I was not a graduate and was the first Southerner to take the job), I framed my inaugural address around quotations from the extant addresses of my twelve predecessors. The continuities in their versions of the Union mission were striking. I quickly perceived that the school had long defined itself around certain polarities: church and academy, evangelical piety and high scholarship, urban locale and international outreach, social reconciliation and social justice. I came to realize that Union's cantankerous history had much to do with the wide scope of its scholarly-practical aspirations, not unique to the world of theological schools but perhaps uniquely intense. Openness to the new was nothing new at Union. In this respect it was liberal. But acknowledging history and the authority of ancient events and ancient documents linked the enterprise to tradition. Henry Sloane Coffin, ninth president, tagged the Union tradition as "liberal evangelical." In the late 1970s, I noted this phrase in a speech to a southern Baptist audience, and a gasp went through the room. By then, the two words had become opposites in popular American church-talk. The issue is one of the more subtle facts about a living religious tradition: its capacity for upsetting tradition. The Hebrew prophets were models of this phenomenon: they discerned tests in tradition that measured the virtues and vices of the present, all the while insisting that unprecedented events in the present were challenges to new forms of repentance.

New presidents must buy into the history of the organization they preside over. Not to study and appropriate its past is to wander blindfolded into its future.

Honoring Prestigious History with New Definitions of Prestige

Union's identification with its history had problems, however. From time to time in speeches, I would remind audiences that a prophetic institution finds ways to repent of its own historical sins. In Union's case, for example, it had sinned by firing a member of the faculty for his German sympathies during World War I, and it did not acknowledge women as eligible for ordained ministers until the 1950s. These were healthy references for the post-1975 generation of faculty, because by then people around the country were asking questions like, "Will the new president restore Union to its glory days under Paul Tillich and Reinhold Niebuhr?" I had to reply to this question by asserting new kinds of "glory" that Union was fashioning in the persons of faculty like James Cone, Beverly Harrison, James Forbes, Cornel West, James Washington, Phyllis Trible, and Kosuke Koyama. I speculated that, if Niebuhr were to return to Union today, he might find fewer students willing to study "under" him and a lot more willing to argue with him. Celebrating past and present with no derogation of either is a delicate presidential task. It was especially so at Union in the 1970s among faculty who had to fight the suggestion that they were no longer intellectuals on a par with their predecessors. Inspiration by an institutional past is one thing; intimidation by it is another.

Overcoming the Split between Educational Aspiration and Financial Constraint

Perhaps the greatest shift in my sense of vocation, in coming to Union, came in my transition from ten years of educational innovation on two university campuses to the unwelcome task of jettisoning innovations pioneered by my predecessors at Union. The fiscal ship was in danger of capsizing. Certain programs—Religion and Drama, Psychiatry and Religion, the Advanced Program in Religious Studies—had been generously funded by foundation grants, which are always time-limited. Eliminating good educational programs went against my personal grain and that of numerous colleagues. Not only could we not afford new untested educational ideas; we could not afford some of the old, tested ideas either. Throwing away cargo is hard for any ship captain; in the process, the thought naturally occurs: how much can we throw away and still be making this voyage worthwhile?

The board and one foundation did help us work on this dilemma by appropriating a fund for educational research, to be spent at the discretion of the president. For the next five years, we tried to sift the best from both the old and the new. A school, dealing with budget cuts, has to keep asking, "What will be the effect on the education of students and the teaching of faculty?" With interviews, experiment, and a lot of discussion, we rediscovered some old educational certainties and envisioned some new ones.

The Ambiguities of Presidential Power

It is a conventional truth that the power of leaders varies with the power attributed to them by constituents. The latter may be ready for the leader to make this or that decision, and in that readiness is a grant of power. At ecumenical, politically feisty Union, however, such grants were rare; in part, I came to believe, because of the diverse theories of church polity in which we all had been raised. Some expected me to be the Episcopal head of the institution, some others the Presbyterian moderator of elected representative leaders, and yet others the Baptist pastor subject to prompt democratic review and recall. This analysis was complicated by other models of authority endemic to the academy, the authority of tenured faculty in particular. After all, faculty are the heart of a school, and that is one reason why a president should be a member of the faculty. Then he can be first among equals, not the unequal convener of superiors. Like most medical doctors, faculty see their daily work as the object of administrative services. They are not shy about denigrating administration as something less than "real work," a phrase that a candid colleague used wryly with me on one occasion. Like many clergy, academics tend to despise administration. A professor's "promotion" to dean or president is widely viewed as a fall from grace. Outsiders may call academic presidents "CEOs," but insiders know how limited is the analogy to heads of business corporations. In academe, hierarchy is flatter. Power accrues from negotiation. And at Union, everybody wanted to be part of the negotiation.

In such an institution, the power of the board of directors is also limited but less ambiguous in the areas for which bylaw and civil law makes them responsible. As a free-standing institution, related to a university but not under its authority, the board legally owns Union Seminary. It is responsible to the state government that chartered the school originally (in 1836) and that still certifies various degree programs. Over time, nothing is more important than a president's powers to influence appointments to the board. But a board is no mirror image of presidential preferences. Its chief, unequivocal right is the appointment and termination of a president. Presidents do not forget that! Important to note here is the role of the board chair. She or he is a true colleague of the president in ways not duplicated by a dean or faculty confidant. Over those sixteen years, I could not have survived without the skills, trust, and advice of two superb board chairmen.

All this adds up to considerable ambiguity of presidential power. Faculties and board members do not always understand each other very well. The achievements of the one are often the fruit of intellectual work that is hard to evaluate numerically. The budgets, including the deficits, that boards approve annually are only too subject to the numbers. The president here is the person in the middle, representative of the faculty to the board and vice versa.

Keeping wisdom flowing in both directions for the making of decisions is a first-order communication challenge.

As he was about to retire from our faculty, Raymond E. Brown, internationally distinguished Catholic scholar of the New Testament, had breakfast with me. One of his parting remarks to me was: "I think that Union runs best when its president is a Presbyterian, and it helps if the president is also a Christian." It was a personally affirmative remark, especially the "Christian." About the Presbyterian side his hunch may have been right, for Presbyterian leaders are accustomed to infinite committee consultations! They are, or ought to be, uncomfortable with unilateral decision-making. But analogies from church government worked only partially at Union. The ambiguity of presidential and every other power never went away. I want to say more about this below, for powerful people in a *theological* school are supposed to count on another Power to imposed limits on their own.

Adjusting the Pace of Change: Too Fast, Too Slow

The 1960s were a tough time for universities and professional schools. Student rioters demanded change in educational aims and methods, and they refused to let the leaders of schools ignore the civil rights movement, the war in Vietnam, and the relation of university interests to the interests of their neighborhoods. Many campuses saw classes coming to a halt, buildings barricaded, and presidents' offices occupied. The Columbia University "bust" of 1968 was a prominent example. Both students and faculty at nearby Union Seminary were in the thick of the upset.

Another essay in this collection reflects on some of the educational lessons I learned from these difficult years. When I arrived at Union in 1975, people on Morningside Heights were sorting out questions about how much change graduate education needs to consider if it means to take contemporary world history into account in its classrooms, finances, and internal life. A certain new sobriety had fallen on the place: change a university or a seminary, and you may not have changed much in the society as a whole. Reject the old traditions of study in the academic disciplines, and you may have thrown out some powerful resources for change. Undermine slow-moving procedures for dealing with conflict, and you may become hostage to chaos. "Make haste slowly" may have been only a half-right adage of the Greeks, but it was not wisdom to be trashed.

Striking a balance between change too-fast and change too-slow will never be easy in any institution, perhaps churches and academic institutions most of all. Their typical activities take time: thinking, study, contemplation, argument, worship, meditation, writing books, questioning old truth, and considering new truth. Time slows down in schools. One task of teachers and administrators is to serve the future by refusing to settle down comfortably in the present.

For an institution whose daily life is fraught with class schedules, attention to stewardship of time can be remarkably low. "Getting through this semester" occupies faculty and students alike. Postponing thought about next year's challenges seems always possible. A certain sense of timelessness haunts the internal culture of bureaucracies large and small: there is always next week, next year. But external society in our time does not respect this fact. It does not wait for institutions to catch up. Suspension in time is dangerous to all organizations. One day their leaders will wake up to find that the times have passed them by.

Getting constituents to think a decade ahead is a struggle, and with the board the president must sponsor that struggle. Ecologists have taught us to think generationally. They tax our minds and our imaginations with the task of taking present account of future beings that we cannot see. Liberation theology asks us to give voice to the voiceless, and by definition the most voiceless of all are members of a generation not yet born. In the years 1975–91, from time to time people would come to our classrooms and faculty who were portents of a coming-on generation: women forty years old seeking a second career, former actors and stock brokers ready to probe the "why" questions, and people born outside the United States convinced that western Christians have something to learn from Africa and Asia. I came to see many of these folk as emissaries from a future to which theological education had better pay attention if it was not to get lost in its past.

Tending the Store vs. Citizenship in the Community

The freedom to become engaged socially is personal to me as a social ethicist. Asked in 1991 what I missed most in my sixteen years as Union president, I said that I missed the freedom I enjoyed while in Raleigh and Atlanta to involve myself in the causes, politics, and secular organizations of the community.

One of the few times when I felt really involved in an issue of justice in the affairs of New York City was a case of police brutality exercised against one of our black students. The case escalated into a large public fracas. I participated in a congressional hearing held in Harlem on police brutality, and it was the only occasion when, to my knowledge, a sound bite from some testimony of mine reached national TV news. The political surge of interest in the city around this issue finally led to the appointment of its first African-American police commissioner, Benjamin Ward.

Early in the twentieth century, a president of the United States (William Howard Taft) journeyed from Washington to New Haven to consult on the appointment of a new dean for Yale Divinity School. That day is long past. Now not even presidents of large universities are expected to be important advocates of public causes or consultants to government. Reinhold Niebuhr was expected to be, but nowadays pastors of megachurches are more likely to be invited to the White House than academic theologians. The more powerful restriction on the public role of educational administrators, however, is simply their first-order responsibility for keeping their institutions alive and well. The money must always be raised, the inside conflicts have to be settled, the work piles up on your desk when you are away. People like to have their president around. "We wish he were here more often," even when, while he is away, he is raising the money that pays for the place.

Stretching Pluralism While Guarding the Coherence of the Institution

As he completed his year with us as a visiting professor in 1977, Eberhard Bethge, premier biographer of Dietrich Bonhoeffer, said to me: "I have never been in a school where people *talked* so much about 'community' and that had so little of it." It was an objective assessment. In the old days of Union, say in the 1930s, almost every student was male, white, and in residence. "Community" in such a group came readily. Now, in the 1990s, with half of our students commuters, half women, and 25 percent members of an ethnic minority, we were a pluralistic place, subject to misunderstandings, hostilities, and caucuses galore. No wonder people complained wistfully about a lack of community. As one black woman put it, "Sometimes in class I want to offer some disagreement with what another student said, but then I think that I'll be slammed against the wall for speaking up, so I keep quiet." She was speaking figuratively (I hope), but hers was nonetheless a worrisome testimony.

Unappreciated in our school and many others, I suspect, is the role of institutional structure, rules, and standard procedures for the expression of conflict. A poignant, delicate example from my time at Union was its increasing affirmation of gay and lesbian students. It was not a clear-cut affirmation. Gay students saw themselves as an oppressed minority in the society at large, and they were quick to pick up signs of rejection from one or another quarter in the school. The result for the president was that he found himself standing between a self-identified oppressed minority and outsiders who thought that it *should* be repressed. My only resolution of the problem was simply to keep on insisting, first of all in my interior self, that kindness and respect towards people different from oneself is the first law of the ethics of Jesus: "Love one another" is prior to discerning each other's sins, alleged or real.

This was one of the junctures where I must say that my most important preparation for being president of a seminary was my experience as pastor of a congregation. Money-raising mounts higher and higher on presidential agendas in the modern world of education, and money can help settle some human conflicts. But only a few. More likely is the reverse: conflicts inside the institution can diminish chances of success in raising much-needed money. Donors to schools strongly resist investing in a war zone. I have always admired one of our generous supporters from the 1970s who respected Union's tradition of honoring freedom of thought. Trouble is, the more such freedom exists within any group, the more likely the social bond will snap.

In my time as president, I had to deal with the criminal behavior of a non-academic staff member, charges against staff of sexual abuse of women students, destructive acting-out of mentally ill students, rumors of spouse abuse, and intra-faculty hostilities left over from the early 1970s that haunted us into the 1980s. On occasion, we dealt with these matters by setting up a new committee for grievances. More often, there was no precedent for settling the conflict in ways that were just, kind, and attentive to the depth of the conflict. I had an administrative colleague at North Carolina State University who borrowed an image from electrical engineering: "You have to put your hands into the brine and feel the currents." Just so: in the face of some crises, one just had to wade in, feel the waves of the fracas, endure the winds of blame that came one's way, and work out compromises that embodied rough, imperfect justice. On many of these occasions, I reflected ruefully how Union Seminary as a human institution acted in ways predicted by the political analysis of its star theologian Reinhold Niebuhr: power conflicts, "moral" people in collision with "immoral" collectives, imperfect settlements of conflicts between imperfect people. I sometimes had to agree with Reiney's brother, H. Richard at Yale, that institutions are custodians of some human goods that can be more ethical than the good of any one individual. It is not always true that "society" is less moral than "moral man."

In all of this, I was sometimes reminded at Union of the great capitalized sentence in the final "Message" of the founding assembly of the World Council of Churches in 1948: "WE INTEND TO STAY TOGETHER." Somebody in an institution had better intend that, the president most of all. Parish ministry helped me respect the leadership that bends towards staying together: not to reply to anger with anger, to wait a while before defensive "setting the record straight," to grant others the freedom to be wrong while on their way to getting it right. An educational community ought to be a learning community! Ought. I was not the only member of the Union community who tried to practice these principles. I always suspected that the best practitioners among my colleagues had learned from the life of the church. Among the most pastoral of my faculty colleagues were historian Robert T. Handy and ethicist Roger L. Shinn. They tell me that theologian Daniel Day Williams belonged solidly to this partnership of reconcilers. His death in 1973, deprived Union of a theologian who, probably more than anyone else in the faculty, took pains to study and appreciate the writings and opinions of his colleagues. Such members of an institution are, in their very selves, the sources of its coherence, integrity, and survival. They are the leaven that often saves the lump.

Being Ethicist and Administrator without Being a Hypocrite

In organizations, "free speech" is a virtue requiring limitation by other virtues. Early in my tenure as president of Union, I learned to curb my ordinary academic habit of speaking my mind—on this, that, and another institutional issue—in conversation with folk in the halls and over the lunch table. A president's thinking-out-loud about yet-to-be-decided policies can lead to trouble. People assume that if you are thinking about doing something, you will do it! At issue here is the importance of collaboration in thinking through any policy question. Without that collaboration, presidential power diminishes. Too many cooks may spoil the broth, but too few cooks may produce a broth that too few others find tasty.

The mellow, smooth-edged rhetoric of politicians has its source in this dilemma. One of their jobs is enabling constituents to stick together while complex policies for dealing with conflicting interests are being worked out. Even if eventually some interests will suffer, it is important not to give any signal ahead of time that the cards are already stacked against them in the all-powerful opinions of the president. The president, of course, is not all that powerful, but folk can imagine him so. Will his casual remarks soon turn into fixed intentions?

Facing One's Own Fallibility and Finitude

In one of his books, Peter Berger comments that all of us grow up thinking that others know more than we know. Then, by chance, one comes into a position of some authority and stumbles over the speculation: "What did my predecessors know and do here? Were they as uncertain and as fallible as am I?" The adult answer is "yes." The second section of Bonhoeffer's poem, "Who Am I?" confesses just this discrepancy between the inner and outer views of the allegedly self-confident leader.

My own version of this discrepancy, not laced with modesty but with realism, was a reflection that ensued from the invitation of the search committee to accept the job. "Does this mean that the other twelve presidents of this place had about the same real but limited competence that the committee now sees in me? Are the institutions of this society run by people more or less of my finite caliber?" These musings were not cover for self-disparagement. It was rather like the anxieties of a Moses and a Jeremiah when called by the Spirit of God to undertake certain threatening responsibilities. To conflate several metaphors from the works of those prophets and the Apostle Paul, one must conclude that God has lots of pots and earthen vessels for carrying around treasure, so that neither overweening pride nor self-derogating modesty should inhibit the faith required to say: "Okay, here am I, send me. Let's try it."

A call in the Calvinist-Presbyterian church tradition, however, requires the confirmation of other instruments of the Spirit. Other people invite you to the job, and then you invite others into the job. Here too is a temptation: if others are responsible for the call, they must share responsibility for your own limitations and mistakes. This form of scapegoating offers only-too-convenient excuses. Some bucks really do stop at the president's desk; and on occasion, presidents must play the role of scapegoats. If you agree to the firing of someone appointed by someone else by consenting to that firing, you bear some blame for it.

The pain of firing anyone, most executives confess, is the most difficult burden of their power. Anyone who enjoys walking into an office to tell someone, "You're fired," does not deserve the power. Similarly, CEO's of large corporations who downsize the organization by eliminating hundreds of jobs do not deserve larger salaries for doing so. Quite the contrary: they could bear some of the pain they impose by bearing some of it by reduction of their salaries, or by refusing a bonus at the end of the year.

Among the most painful experiences of finitude for corporate presidents has to be their failure to increase company sales and stock values to levels that they and their boards hope for. The experience of not-for-profit presidents is similar in our failure to raise annual contributions and endowment sufficient for maintaining and improving next year's mission. A professional by definition knows her or his limits. Robert Browning offered some comfort in the line, "A man's reach must exceed his grasp, else what's a heaven for?" A reader of the New Testament could amend that to: ". . . or what's an eschaton for?" In the more mundane context of a president's life, a more sober version might be: "One administration's reach must exceed its grasp, else what's the next administration for?"

Deciding When to Resign

Long presidencies have benefits—mine was sixteen years, twice the average for American seminary presidents. Building institutional strength requires more than a year or two. John Fletcher advised me in 1975, "Don't take the job unless you're willing to spend ten years at it."

The difficulty of that rule is that it may disguise the rhythms and cycles of need and opportunity in the life of the institution. My last six years at Union were much taken up with crucial shifts in our struggle with a structural deficit, focused on the dangers of too much withdrawal from the endowment. Somehow the hand of duty drew me "once more into the breach" of a problem I now understood as well as anyone else around.

There are dangers and downsides to the lure of duty, however. In spite of vision and ambition, no president solves all the problems. Every solution that one has helped invoke has its cost in loss of support of people who did not like the solution; for example, a cost-cutting decision to move faculty out of one apartment and into another. Every year most leaders lose some friends. Popularity erodes, an ordinary phenomenon in the career of almost every politician. A leader can be sure of certain achievements, but just as sure is the much-left-to-achieve. This thought opens one to the realism that "There are gifts needed in this time of history that I do not possess." Equally realistic is admitting to oneself that some aspects of the job are getting old. For me, two in particular: the same old human conflicts walking through the door, and the same old financial needs never quite met. That both were "old" was a signal from my psyche that it was time to retire.

But retirement as president did not mean retirement from education or from its heart, teaching. All during those sixteen years as president, I had taught at least one academic course per year and had developed inter-professional courses in five neighboring schools of our Morningside Heights community. It was a sideline vital for the flow of my intellectual and spiritual juices in the midst of budgets, committees, and money-raising travel. I had never let lapse the inter-professional teaching dimension of my calling. So, with ready board consent, I accepted four years of fulltime teaching to round out a twenty-one year tenure at Union. In recent years, a number of academic presidents have done the same. I was pleased to initiate the precedent at Union.

The Theology I Tried to Practice

It behooves the leaders of theological schools to think theologically about their jobs. This is risky, first because many aspects of the job are quite comparable to those of administrators in secular organizations. There, theology may be as pertinent as it is in an institution that has the word "theos" in its title. A belief in the priesthood of all believers and divine presence in all of life should yield such pertinence. Moreover, many times I have thought *politically* about the work of pastors and church executives. There is good Calvinist precedent for that thinking. As Sheldon Wolin put it, Calvin developed both a religious theory of the state and a political theory of the church.

My chief worry about heavy theologizing about the job is the danger of baptizing this and that finite event with the allegation "Deus vult!" That was the slogan of the first Crusade of 1099 under the influence of Pope Gregory VII, one of the truly disastrous events of Christian-Muslim history. Theological seminaries abound with students and faculty inclined to legitimate their interests with divine blessing. Proof-texts fill the air and "compromise" is seen as a betrayal of faith and ethics. The Apostle advised the Roman Christians "not to think of oneself more highly than one ought to think, but to think with sober judgment . . ." (Romans 12:3). Not bad advice for the politics of theological seminaries if its leaders mean it when they ponder theology like the following.

Education Will Not Save the World, Not Even Theological Education, Which Should Teach that God Saves It

The first of the Ten Commandments (Exodus 20:3) forbids idolatry, and a seminary with an international reputation is a good place to forbid it. Part of the pain of budget cutbacks in my era was the sense, shared by many graduates, that Union was too great an institution to suffer such constrictions. Shades of the 2009 recession: not too big to fail, but too aligned with the purposes of God to fail! When, in the mid-1980s, we actually voiced in our board the possibility that a freestanding liberal theological New York school might have to go out of business, the Calvinism in me had to consent anew to the faith that God could rule the world without the assistance of Union Seminary. The positive implication underneath this negative is the importance of a human institution that embraces just this doctrine. Dietrich Bonhoeffer expressed it beautifully and poignantly when, with his hope of a career as a scholarly theologian cut short by imprisonment, he acknowledged that the best humans can do is to offer to God and the future a fragment of faithful work that God, in turn, can compose into Her own designs, like those of a master-weaver or stained-glass-window maker or Bach's *Art of Fugue*.[2]

New Occasions Teach New Definitions of Excellence and Prestige

The era 1975–91 saw some astonishing changes in the 200+ seminaries in the United States. Among the most dramatic was the coming of second career students from the worlds of business, art, government, and especially homes, where women came to believe that God did not mean to limit ministers to men. By the 1980s, Union's enrollment of women in its degree programs equaled that of men. To the new, articulate mix of students came African-Americans, Hispanics, members of churches in Africa and Asia, and persons of diverse sexual self-identity. Union had long prided itself on hospitality to "all sorts and conditions" of human concerns. Its location in New York City in 1836 was innovative in a time when theological seminaries preferred the insulations of the countryside. In my time, varieties of religious experience and diversities of culture seemed too much to integrate into a curriculum, a budget, a faculty, and a score of teaching methods. At these times the old adage, "Beware of being the first to change," haunted us. Did we really want to be known as the place of welcome to so many lifestyles, theologies, and career hopes?

Yes we did, and we had to sense the vigor of human relations in our classes and caucuses as signs of the more universal humanity to which the God and Father of Jesus was inviting us all. We had always been a feisty place into which students and faculty freely brought their differences. Appreciating, working out, and looking for touches of the divine Spirit even in clashes over interpretations of that Spirit, came close to the essence of our ecumenical place. It was not a comfortable place sometimes. It was often a place intensely alive with new insight into what it means to believe that we all belong in the circle of our Creator's love.

Leaders are Servants, Not Heroes

Leaders grow when they listen, risk vulnerability, and are not embarrassed to change their minds. If professing Christians, they remember that the New Testament word for repentance is *metanoia*, a life-comprehending change of mind.

I like what Max Dupree said about leaders: "The first duty of a leader is to define reality. The last is to say 'thank you.' In between the leader is a servant." That first duty is not easy to pursue. T.S. Eliot observed, "Humankind cannot bear very much reality." That applies to presidents, too. For example, it took me five years to feel that I understood the realities of Union's budget problems, often against much resistance from students and faculty who did not want to perceive the problems.

Much easier to enact is Dupree's third rule. I tried to say "thank you" a lot in those sixteen years, following the habit for which President George H.W. Bush was well known. He sent off numerous little "thank you" notes. I wrote thousands of them.

The duty to be a servant is the most ambiguous. A trusted staff member at Union once said to me, "You know, you brought two great gifts to us as president. One was that you absorbed so much hostility." (The other, he added, was an astonishing marriage—another matter, but it was significant that he thought it significant. I thought so, too.) I had to reflect that, in a community that celebrates righteous anger at injustice, it is important for the stability of the place that somebody reins in their capacity for anger. Leaders had better privatize some of their own anger in response to that of others. If they angrily align themselves with one faction in a conflict, they decrease their ability to help put the community back together.

More required than restraining one's anger is openness to learning from many sides of a conflict how in action to take account of many perceived interests. The line between wise flexibility and supine pliability is hard to draw. Frequently, it nevertheless has to be drawn. Not all issues yield to compromise, not all majorities deserve presidential support, nor do all mind-changes deserve the name of repentance. On the other hand, mind-change is painful, necessary business. Leaders had better develop their capacity for that pain.

Perhaps the true underlying theological-ethical issue here is how one acquires the "broken and contrite heart" of Psalm 51 while having to take stands, announce decisions, and shoulder aggressive initiatives. Seminaries can be full of folk who, in Learned Hand's phrase, only irregularly exhibit "the spirit of liberty that is not too sure it is right." Presidents should pray for the gift of that spirit. H. Richard Niebuhr of Yale once remarked that "we all have a right to views of the absolute, but none of us has a right to absolute views." Early in my years at Union, it seemed that arrogance sometimes controlled the spirits of the place, and I prayed that I would not imitate it. The great, faithful control of human arrogance, of course, is an awareness of our creature-hood and sin. I confess some difficulty here, for not all the sins of which this president was accused was I willing to confess as real sins! But there were plenty of real ones to confess. For dealing with them, the forgiveness of God and colleagues (see Psalm 51) was much in order. Over the years, I had many occasions to insist, along with Jesus' teaching about prayer in Matthew 6:9–15, that horizontal forgiveness belongs integrally to the vertical in the Christian life. Many times, too, I had confirmed in my own experience the view of secular philosopher Hannah Arendt that societies change with the coming of two powerful shared decisions: agreement on new standards, laws, and constitutions for the future; and forgiveness of the mistakes of the past. Arendt gave Jesus credit for discovering the indispensable power of forgiveness for dealing with social wrongs of the past. She would have agreed with Robert Frost, "To be social is to be forgiving." I found forgiveness at Union Seminary a much more practical, down-to-earth social virtue than Reinhold Niebuhr seems to have found it. Niebuhr knew the theological importance of human repentance. One of his biographers titled her book, *The Courage to Change.* To that virtue, I would add: the courage to forgive and to be forgiven.

Like the Christian Life, Leadership Is a Journey, a Pilgrimage, Not "Management by Objectives"

I end with an extended explanation, in theological terms, of the difference between leadership and "management by objectives."

In their book, *Leadership and Ambiguity: The American College Presidency*, Michael D. Cohen and James G. March challenge the popular, modern rationalist paradigm of organizational leadership, "Management by Objectives." What if responsible management consists of pursuit of certain objectives in expectation of finding better ones? Rational thinking about acting assumes that one identifies goals and then pursues them, devising means to fit the ends. Suppose our goals are incomplete at best and wrong at worst?

> Perhaps we should explore . . . how we ought to behave when our value premises are not yet (and never will be) fully determined. Suppose we treat action as a way of creating goals at the same time as we treat goals as a way of justifying action.
>
> ———————————
>
> Interesting people and interesting organizations construct complicated theories of themselves. To do this, they need to supplement the technology of reason with the technology of foolishness. Individuals and organizations sometimes need ways of doing things for which they have no good reason. They need to act before they think.

Cohen and Marsh go on to comment that "in an organization that wants to continue to develop new objectives, a manager needs to be tolerant of the idea that he will discover the meaning of yesterday's action in the experiences and interpretations of today." The corollaries are several: goals can be mere hypotheses; intuition may serve us better on occasion than goals; the ability to "forget and overlook" may be as important as memory; and past experience may need to remain open to new understanding. "Experience can be changed retrospectively. By changing our interpretative concepts now, we modify what we learned earlier. Thus we expose the possibility of experimenting with alternative histories."[3]

The ability to change experience retrospectively fits my own vocational journey from a local pastorate, to an experimental program of multi-disciplinary studies in a university, to teaching in a theological seminary, to becoming president of one. It certainly embodies a very careful, even bold philosophy of pragmatism. But more, for me it comports closely with statements about two leaders in the New Testament.

> He [Jesus] learned obedience through what he suffered. (Hebrews 5:8)

> He [Abraham] went out, not knowing where he was to go. (Hebrews 11:8)

In the going, both believed that trustworthy guidance would be given to them along the way.

I can think of many illustrations of how certain positive events in my Union years validated for me this pilgrimage-image of work, leadership, and change. Two stand out.

Soon after arriving at Union, I observed with surprise the baleful impact of budget constrictions on the ecumenical breadth of its curriculum and student body. Money for scholarships for international students was in scarce supply, and the great ecumenical tradition of Henry Pitt Van Dusen and John Bennett seemed under threat. As one boost to that tradition, we appointed a new professor of ecumenics, first Robert McAfee Brown and then Kosuke Koyama. With generous funding from the Luce Foundation, we opened the windows of the seminary onto the world church in the form of academic courses and support of visiting scholars from three continents. It was a timely initiative. Soon the wider world of America's 200 theological seminaries, through their Association of Theological Schools, formed a committee to study "The Globalization of Theological Education," making me the chair and Koyama a member of the committee. Six years later, the ATS formally adopted accreditation standards that required its schools to include in their training of ministers and scholars global perspectives.

A fruit of these developments was insistence in the standards on more than book-learning about our world neighbors. That is why, in early 1992, Professor Koyama and I found ourselves in southern Africa participating in a "global-local immersion" in the life of people who were both different from us and akin to us. We spent two days in a Zimbabwe village and in an all-night worship service of the local "New African" congregation. On another occasion, Koyama and I spent a night in Tembisa, a township outside Johannesburg, as guests of Christians in their "informal" houses that Americans would call shacks. I will never forget how the father and mother of my hostfamily loaned their bedroom to me for the night and prepared a dinner of chicken and vegetables that must have strained their food budget. Nor will I forget the meeting we had next morning with the council of neighborhood leaders in which we shared our hopes that one day my white skin and their black skin would no longer be badges of different human identities.

It is easy to be aware of global humanity in a city like New York. I was agreeably surprised to see that awareness develop in American theological schools as a whole. Union helped catalyze this development, and in turn we benefitted from it. We discovered some new goals from this experience. It was not an example of "management by objectives."

A more dramatic and even more gratifying illustration of where the pilgrim spirit can lead is the fifteen year course of events that resulted in the establishment of Union's new endowed chair of theology in the name of Dietrich Bonhoeffer. In the early 1960s, his *Letters and Papers from Prison* undergirded a number of my efforts at North Carolina State University to find God and the church "in the center of the village." Bonhoeffer became for me the most important European theologian, chiefly because his life and thought were so immersed in the great political crises of my own youth during the years 1930–45. Reading the great Bethge biography in 1977 was the spiritual height of that summer, and my address to the International Bonhoeffer Society in 1984 clarified my reasons for believing that his theology and life were models of Christian fidelity in the midst of colossal evildoing by political leaders and citizens of one's own country.

Bonhoeffer had been a student at Union in the academic year 1930–31. He returned to New York for three weeks in the summer of 1939. That latter visit was consumed with the decision whether to return to Germany and the certain onset of war. The Union guest room in which he stayed for those weeks had the name "prophet's chamber." We know that he probably made his decision to return to Germany in that room. As he left to board the last passenger ship to leave New York harbor for Germany, he wrote a note to Reinhold Niebuhr, who was urging him to wait out the war in America.

> I will have no right to participate in the
> reconstruction of Christian life in Germany
> after the war if I do not now share the trials
> of this time with my people . . . .[4]

So he returned to Berlin, joined the resistance to Hitler, and paid the price for doing so with his execution on April 9, 1945, in the Flossenberg concentration camp.

In 1975, the Prophet's Chamber at Union was a rather disheveled place where tutors could hang their hats and keep their papers. A member of our board (UTS, '65) agreed to refurbish the room with a gift of $25,000. It turned into a choice space for classes, faculty and board meetings, and special events. We promptly named it the Bonhoeffer Room, and for its dedication during a ceremony in the room, we awarded Eberhard Bethge our fourth Union Medal.

On Second Thought

It was a very significant ceremony, bringing together history, theology, and prophetic contemporary Christian witness. But the end was not yet. In June 1989, as the Tiananmen Square demonstrations erupted in Beijing and five months before the fall of the Berlin Wall, we awarded the Union Medal to Richard F. Von Weizsaecker, president of the Federal Republic of Germany, in tribute to the courageous address that he delivered to the Bundestag on May 8, 1985, on the fortieth anniversary of the end of war in Europe. In that hour-long speech, he did what few politicians dare to do: publicly exposing in detail the crimes of predecessors.

> . . . [T]he six million Jews who were murdered
> . . . the unthinkable number of citizens of the
> Soviet Union and Poland . . . our own
> countrymen . . . the murdered Sinti and Roma .
> . . the homosexuals . . . the mentally ill . . .
> the hostages . . . the Resistance in all countries
> . . . the German resistance . . . [and all those]
> who accepted death rather than humble their
> consciences. . . .

As a lieutenant in Hitler's *Wehrmacht*, Weizsaecker confessed that he bore some responsibility for these crimes. He warned his listeners against "arrogance and self-righteousness."

> We learn from our own history what man
> is capable of. . . . As human beings we have
> learned, as human beings we remain
> endangered. . . . Our request to young people
> is this: Do not allow yourselves to be driven
> into enmity and hatred against other people,
> against Russians and Americans, against Jews
> or Turks, against radicals or conservatives,
> against black or white. . . .[5]

There was no more fitting memorial to the likes of Dietrich Bonhoeffer than this speech forty years after 1945. Bonhoeffer had died in hope of saving his country from great evil. Political leaders like von Weizsaecker sustained that hope. There was no better place at Union for acknowledging all of this than the Bonhoeffer Room.

The end of this Bonhoeffer-inspired journey was still not yet. In the early 1990s some of us wondered: would some group of German church and business leaders help Union to endow a faculty chair in the name of Bonhoeffer? The answer was a stronger "yes" than most of us dared believe. By 1994, German and American donors raised an endowment of one and a half million dollars for a professorship, an associated lectureship, and an annual exchange of scholars. In the midst of this effort, in my last year as president, one board member, Joseph Robinson, first oboist of the New York Philharmonic, proposed that we sponsor a "Heroes of Conscience" memorial symphonic concert. For conductor of the concert, we sought the leadership of Christoph von Dohnanyi, music director of the Cleveland Symphony and son of the resistance leader Hans von Dohnanyi, who was executed in the same week as Bonhoeffer. The concert came to pass at the Riverside Church on April 5, 1992. With Robinson's and Dohnanyi's recruiting, members of the orchestra came from the first chairs of orchestras from a dozen countries, including Israel, England, and Germany. National Public Radio broadcast the concert and subsequently one hundred PBS stations repeated the broadcast. Numbers of our Jewish neighbors came. All 3000 seats of that Gothic church were filled. With the help of Brahms, Beethoven, Schoenberg, Arvo Paert, Hermann Prey, Gidon Kramer, Bill Moyers, and Joseph Flummerfelt, we experienced that Sunday afternoon a marvelous knitting-together of twentieth century historical crisis, prophetic Christian courage, high art, and theology wrung out of suffering. The New York Choral Artists performed the *German Requiem*. Moyers read from the Bonhoeffer letters. Some of the musicians said it was the most important performance of their lives.

I had resigned from the Union presidency ten months before the event. During the rehearsal on Saturday, I stood for a moment in the center aisle of the church and reflected how a president's efforts over time are cluttered with many false starts and sheer failures. Yet, some successes do come, and they have about them an air of divine grace. They are more a happening than anyone's personal achievement. I knew, in all candor, that this thread of success in honoring Bonhoeffer at Union would not have happened without me; but, as my German colleague Helmut Reihlen (chief fundraiser for the project in Germany) said to me at the end of a visit with him in Berlin: "We must remember that we are succeeding in this because of Bonhoeffer, not because of us." Had Bonhoeffer himself been there to join the conversation, he would probably have added, "Because of God's grace, not Bonhoeffer's." He might have reminded us of a passage from a 1944 letter about our privilege of being "a fragment in the hands of God."Presidents of all sorts need some successes, interspersed among the failures, to encourage them to "keep on keeping on." When success happens, they are dull of soul if they do not exclaim, "Thank God!"

NOTES

1 This and the following pages of this essay are adapted from a longer 1996 essay of mine, "The President As Pilgrim," written at the request of the Association of Theological Schools in the United States and Canada and published (as one of six similar essays by seminary presidents of the era) in a special issue of the ATS Journal, *Theological Education: Leadership, the Study of the Seminary Presidency, Reflections of Seminary Leaders* (Volume XXXII, Supplement III, 115–51), edited by Neely D. McCarter. The study was funded by the Lilly Endowment. I thank ATS for permission to adapt the latter third of my essay there to the essay here. The quotation above comes from page 126 of that longer version.

2 *Letters and Papers from Prison*: Enlarged Edition. Ed. Eberhard Bethge (New York: The Macmillan Company, 1971), 219, letter of February 23, 1944. "The important thing today is that we should be able to discern from the fragment of our life how the whole was arranged and planned, and what material it consists of . . . their completion can only be a matter for God, so they are fragments which must be fragments."

3 James G. Marsh and Michael D. Cohen, *Leadership and Ambiguity: The American College President*, 2nd edition (Boston: Harvard Business School Press, 1986), 222–28.

4 See Eberhard Bethge, *Dietrich Bonhoeffer: Man of Vision, Man of Courage* (New York: Harper & Row, 1977), 599.

5 Cf. a longer analysis of this historic address in my book *An Ethic for Enemies: Forgiveness in Politics* (New York: Oxford University Press, 1995), 108–12. Original text provided me by the embassy of the Federal Republic of Germany, May 1985.

Chapter 9

Devices of the Mind and Heart: Money

What the conquistadors failed to understand
is that money is a matter of belief, even faith
in the person paying us; belief in the person
issuing the money he uses or the institution
that honours his cheques or transfers. Money
is not metal. It is trust inscribed.

—*Niall Ferguson*[1]

I remember vividly the first dollar bill that I felt I owned: an allowance to me from my father when I was nine years old. The dollar came with conditions: I was to spend half of it for school lunches, a dime a day for five days a week; twenty-five cents was to be saved in a barrel-bank with "2 percent interest" printed on the bottom; and twenty-five cents went for contributions to our local Methodist church. Soon after, I acquired a bank savings book for recording the times when I deposited that barrel of quarters to people in banks. They worked in buildings downtown that looked like fortresses. Their offices and their demeanors wore all the signs of trustworthiness. That was before banks changed their image to that of businesses with big advertising budgets and depositor premium rewards like toasters.

Some nine-year-olds in 2010 will be incredulous at this early discipline of my father for teaching me the proper uses of money. A miserly allowance? Not so miserly when one notes that, in the mid-1930s, that dollar was worth $14 in contemporary cost-of-living terms. More striking for me in retrospect is the deal struck between my father and me that I would allocate a fourth of that dollar to the church and another fourth to saving. An occasional milk shake or comic book? Not applicable: there were better uses of scarce money in the depths of the Great Depression.

In those years, not a single day passed in our middle class home when my sister and I would go hungry. The Depression touched us but did not greatly damage us. No bread lines for the children of my father, the first college graduate in his family.

The next great leap in my life as spender of money came from what I earned as a morning paperboy. I had a route during the four years between ages fourteen and eighteen. My neighborhood customers numbered about one hundred. From each paper I delivered between 5 A.M. and 7 A.M., 364 days a year, I earned one cent, two cents on the thick Sunday paper, for a total of $8 a week. It was wartime, and putting savings into government bonds was the patriotic thing to do, a precedent that followed me as an army draftee. (I spent one fourth of my army private's monthly income of $75 on helping the government to pay for that very income. In retrospect, that patriotic devotion still astonishes me!) War bonds included, most of that $8 a week during those high school years was mine to spend. The luxury I chiefly spent it on was a collection of classical music, some seventy or eighty 78 rpm albums. I am not sure that my parents always understood that growing enthusiasm in me. But they knew that the eighth grade music teacher who first introduced me to that repertoire must have been a very effective teacher. Those purchases clearly demonstrated that money for me had uses quite transcendent of bread and butter. To earn only enough to keep one's body alive, with nothing left over to feed one's soul, became my implicit understanding of real poverty.

It would be a few years before I learned the term "Protestant Ethic" or John Wesley's version of it: "Earn all you can, save all you can, give all you can." My Methodist parents practiced that ethic, though with certain exceptions. By deciding to put his professional training as a lawyer to the service of our local city government, my father never expected earnings comparable with those of most lawyers in pre- or post-war America. In a decision that still inspires me, he accepted a job that might have qualified as the worst depression-era job in the City Hall of Norfolk, Virginia: Director of Delinquent Taxes. From time to time, he would bring home stories of how little and how much his staff would try to collect from the legion of folk whose taxes were in arrears. In his conversations with some of those folk, he developed a reputation for an ability to quiet anxiety and anger in fellow citizens. From the church and from southern culture, he somehow had acquired arts of interpersonal relations that made him a peacemaker in the best sense of the word. Forty years later, when I became president of a seminary, I remembered that ability in him as ethically and practically important in all organizations.

I have no doubt, therefore, that from those early years I inherited certain dispositions in regard to earning and spending money that have marked me as a child of the Great Depression: spend money on "necessities" not indulgences, stay within your income, save as much of it as possible, always give some away even when you are relatively poor, avoid borrowing except when it is utterly necessary, think always about the proverbial "rainy day," remember needs of people you become responsible for, and— the most life-shaping rule of all—accept work in the not-for-profit human service sector without worrying about its wealth-generating potential for your long-range future. Absent from these rules was one engine of capitalism: borrow money to make money.

It turned out that the woman who agreed to marry me in 1953 also agreed with the same philosophy. "Economy" derives from a Greek word for "household management." We managed our household more or less in accord with these rules. During my first three years of fulltime employment (as a local Presbyterian minister), we not only lived within our $6,000 annual income[2] but saved $1,000 a year. Those savings would later provide almost three years of tuition for my doctoral work at Harvard. The GI Bill had paid for three of my college years. With generous help from fellowships, we finished those Harvard years with no debts, a new job, and a memorable $18 in the bank.

In 2009 most college and graduate students will read this account as a tale told by a guy living in an ancient economic age. Not to be obscured in the story were forms of *investment in me* from the work of others in the American economy: rich philanthropists and government leaders convinced that business profits and taxes should support education.

I was a lucky fellow, yes? By what mixture of luck and prudence, I must let others judge. For purposes of this essay, I want to explore the meaning of the commanding fact that a lot of other people were investing in institutions devoted to the education of the likes of me. It took a rich twentieth century society to send me to school, from kindergarten to Harvard, over a stretch of twenty-five years. I pair my awareness of this personal good fortune with the reminder that a third of the world's population tries to live on a daily dollar worth 1/14 of my dollar in the 1930s. The facts haunt me: the injustice of world poverty in the midst of world wealth. I see from a recent documentary that, among the millions of the world's children who lack primary schooling, half live in Africa. Teachers who go there to help remedy this world-class version of injustice caution their supporters: "You can't teach reading, writing, and arithmetic to hungry children. Without breakfast, they cannot learn." That testimony is a reminder that poverty is a multi-dimensional reality. It is easy in a wealthy society like America, the wealthiest society in history, to forget the importance of breakfast. Back in the 1960s, Harvey Cox talked with a young unemployed woman in Haight Asbury in San Francisco. He asked her how, with no money, she managed to secure bread to eat. She was puzzled at the question. "Bread? Why bread just *is!*" People of my generation are not likely to entertain that illusion, nor can most of global humanity. First of all, work and money are about producing and consuming food enough to feed hungry mouths. Happy are the Americans who can assume that they will never have to experience real hunger, and that they will have at least some money to spend on music, books, and a day at the beach.

The wonderful historical convenience of money is that its possessor can search for neighbors who have food enough for their own mouths and that sufficient food is left over to sell. To the evolution of systems for producing and selling the surpluses of agriculture, beginning at least 5,000 years ago, we moderns owe debts that call for a lot of gratitude to our unknown entrepreneurial ancestors. To make cities possible, they had to invent farms and new systems of exchange. They had to imagine their way out of a barter economy. Readers of Niall Ferguson's *The Ascent of Money* finish the book with new awareness of how routinely we depend on what John Maynard Keynes called "the immaterial devices of the mind" of past generations.[3] They devised economic systems by which some would prosper while others would be put at risk of new forms of starvation. In virtually all their devices, so routine for us, hide historical debates over the good, the bad, and the indifferent things of human economics. Call it an argument over ethics, or the purposes and rules that ought to govern human relations. In this little essay, I want to sketch how the argument continues today in my mind in the midst of The Great Recession of 2007–2009.

Education for What?

Most of the students whom one encountered in business schools in the 1980s had a ready answer to the question of why they were attending school: to make money. An ethics professor had to wait a while before many in the class would ponder the irony in the life stories of their capitalist mentors: Make enough millions on the stock market to retire at thirty-five, and then what? Buy a baseball team? Travel the world, feast on the arts of the Renaissance in Florence? Collect high-priced paintings of impoverished geniuses like Vincent van Gogh? Get a Ph.D. in ecology, political science, philosophy, or theology? Or stay in the game of making more and more money ad infinitum and then, finally, plan to endow one of those liberal arts institutions that educate people like Donald Shriver?

Some years ago the president of the Georgia Institute of Technology reported that his graduates tended to come back for continuing education in three stages. Five years out, they want to keep up with the latest technologies. Ten to fifteen years out, they want to study psychology and social theory, for by then they were mid-level managers and "people persons." Finally, twenty-five years out, many were senior managers who wanted to study philosophy and ethics. They were face-to-face with the big question: What's it all about? In spite of the lures of money, they were beginning to wonder, with John Maynard Keynes, if "love of money" was justifiable apart from the possibility that it could lead to a "good life." As Keynes recent biographer, Robert Skidelsky, put it: For Keynes, "To make the world ethically better was the only justifiable purpose of economic striving."[4] The most reflective of business school students in the 1980s knew that money-making prepares the makers to pursue other purposes. They were not necessarily duped by the 1997 dictum of Jeffrey Skilling that "all that matters is money. . . . This touchy-feely stuff isn't as important as cash. That's what drives performance."[5]

The irony here is that by 1997 Mr. Skilling was already drowning in a flood of "immaterial devices of the mind" for making a lot of money for Enron, most of them closer to the "touchy-feely" reality of greed than any actual benefits to the people of California. Most ironic of all, one of those mental devices,the law, finally drove Mr. Skilling to prison. In the end, Skilling lived in a country whose legal system depends on the counter-dictum that not everything in human life is up for sale. Human worth and human obligation cannot be reduced to cash value. All religions teach this simple, evident truth. They teach it, not out of some philosophic stratosphere, but because of the empirical truth that humans do not live by bread or money-making alone.

Just Prices?

Some years ago a CEO of a large manufacturing plant, a member of a business ethics discussion group, tested my economic ethics with the question: "If I can manufacture something for five cents and sell it for a dollar, is there anything wrong with that?"

It could only be wrong if one asserts some other basis for setting prices than what the market will bear. Capitalism's living dogma is: until competitors force the price down, producers should be free to make a killing. Once alive, now dead: the idea of a "just price."

I am not sure it is altogether dead. Many exceptions to the tyranny of markets, what George Soros called "market fundamentalism," creep into the views of modern business leaders and their publics. Competition feels good to those who are winning, less so for the losers. "Market price" advocates retreat a bit when with each other they agree on a "fair price," calculated as the price which protects profits all around. The term "cutthroat" enters the rhetorical air when good people and good products come under fire from aggressive competitors who take no prisoners. In the public at large, the ghost of just pricing appears when the well-supplied hoard scarce necessities or charge atrocious prices for the same. Orthodox marketers will say: When famine comes, why restrict the profits of those who have food to sell? What's wrong with tripling the price of food after the Katrina hurricane in New Orleans? It's just supply and demand. To ask for any other basis for price is to resort to some "touchy-feely" rule like attention to need as well as to the ability to pay, or compassion as the protector of some vital human relationships.

In the midst of the Great Recession of 2007–2009, the most notorious of objections to the iron law of competition, or Joseph Schumpeter's "creative destruction," have come from failing businesses whose leaders have reached out for massive survival help from national government. Their arguments for survival resound with assertions of "too big to fail," for, they say, our collapse will harm huge numbers of people inside and outside of our companies. A notion of common good has crept into this rhetoric. For the common good, government and taxes should help protect big business from collapse.

So it goes: brave ideologues change when faced with catastrophe. Modern American capitalists should long since have admitted that, without the supports of government and certain legal limits on competition, few businesses would survive. After 9/11/01 in New York City, some numbed leaders of financial institutions, headquartered in the World Trade Center, remarked soberly to journalists: "You know, we walk down the street now more aware of the preciousness of ourselves and other people around us. We still want to make money, but somehow it's not everything." It was very old wisdom, lost on ideologues like Jeff Skilling and Ayn Rand: "A human life does not consist in abundance of possessions" (Luke 12:15). So patently true to experience were those words of Jesus that one should be almost embarrassed to have to repeat them to either the rich or the poor. For me and my house, the most abundant, life-enhancing of my "possessions" happens to be my fifty-six-year-old marriage. We needed money to survive that long. But such a marriage has never been "buy-able" or "assess-able" by measures of money. In a truly human economy, there is such a thing as being priceless. We finally expelled slavery from this American society because we repented of our sin of believing that human beings could be put up for sale.

In 2010, economists and business leaders should be loudly reminding each other and the public that ethical guides to human behavior are as important for economic health as a proper diet is for physical health. Without institutional sanctions against gross affronts to the common good, societies dissolve into Thomas Hobbes's famous "war of all against all." When she fled the Soviet Union for America and became the arch-priestess of individualistic striving for wealth-accumulation, Ayn Rand rejected the collective ethic of communism but kept the materialism and atheism. The philosophy "all that matters is money" owes much to corrupted Marxism, an irony lost on many an enthusiast for the capitalistic system.[6]

So, in the midst of disasters which this recession is visiting on millions of folk worldwide, some of us are returning, grudgingly, to simple truths that somehow got drowned in tides of capital flows, leveraged buyouts, and other "innovative investment vehicles" sweeping over the world of markets. These few simple truths are worth writing about, even though in their simplicity they are likely to prompt the sophisticated to accuse the writer of utter naiveté.

Lying and stealing

Late in the 1980s, the School of Business at Columbia University was visited by a business leader recently released from federal prison. He was fulfilling the "community service" part of his sentence for fraudulent sales of bonds, a crime for which his partner Ivan Boesky was also serving time. In his talk to a special gathering of business students, our visitor stressed his discovery of a major reason for obeying laws: "Prison is no fun. You don't want to risk going to prison. Better obey the law." Ethicists know that this is the oldest minimum reason for ethical behavior: fear of bad consequence. Doing right because it is right—in principle—calls for higher motivation. This is a distinction made by Catholic penitential doctrine between attrition and contrition. Happily, in the discussion period, certain students raised the question, "Do you ever think regretfully about all those investors, some of them widows living on pensions, who lost money from your work in bonds?" "Well, no." came the reply. "After all the losses were spread thin over thousands of investors. No one of them suffered much."

The students did not find that opinion very convincing. From somewhere, they had acquired the notion that consequences—and who bears them—matter in law, ethics, and economics. "Do no harm" may be as important in business as in medicine. Impressive to me, and ridiculously ironic, was our visitor's resort to a negative form of *distributive* justice: spread the injustice around, and the consequences are not so terrible.

Nothing afflicts American debates over the economic meaning of the word "justice" so much as our cultural disposition to apply the word chiefly to individuals rather than to their relationships. "Everyone deserves to keep the money he or she earns. My money; it's my money." Cutting through and across this dogma is difficult for us Americans. We came to these shores in flight from cages of law, custom, class, and privilege that clamped shut on the pursuit of wealth by "nobodies." Perhaps nothing drove those millions of Europeans across the Atlantic so powerfully as—not religion——but hunger for land. Down to today, land possession is close to absolute among most of us. We begrudge restrictions on how we can use land. Most of all we quarrel over the taxes. To be tagged as "liberal" in this society, all one has to say is, "We need higher taxes." The loud outcry that greets that view expresses a form of liberalism quite opposed to *liberality*: one should be free to spend one's money without restriction. So much for Wesley's "give all you can."

"Liberal" democracies build barriers against uninhibited exercise of human greed. That's why the Skillings and the Boeskys of our era have gone to jail. Massively and mysteriously silhouetted in the Great Recession of 2007–2009, the legal barriers against limitless greed are not enough. Beyond law there is ethics, an "overplus" of rules for human behavior that cannot ever be captured completely in law and custom but that are sometimes even more important for restraining the ancient sins of greed and sharp practice. We like to boast that as a "free" society we leave some realms of human behavior to the discretion of decisions by individuals and groups. In doing so, we are not leaving ethics behind. The more real the freedom, the more need for ethics.

Amid the corporate scandals of the 1980s and 1990s, I once remarked to my co-teacher James Kuhn: "Perhaps we need more stress on some simple basics. Maybe instead of filling our classes with complex cases of ethical decision in business management, we should have arranged to stretch a big banner across the facade of the B-School with the words, 'THOU SHALT NOT STEAL.' And a second banner, 'THOU SHALT NOT BEAR FALSE WITNESS.'"

Kuhn frequently began our ethics course by reminding students of a symbol that graced that facade for many years: the old Roman symbol for Mercury, god of messages, travel, and trade, but also of trickery. It was a reminder of the ancient, classical suspicion of commerce as a human occupation. American culture has done its best to overturn that prejudice, but the current recession might bring the idea back into fashion. Ordinary consumers are asking if "innovative financial instruments" are innovative ways to steal and lie. Over recent years, we had scarcely come to understand the meaning of "arbitrage" before our minds blurred at talk about derivatives, mortgage bundling, credit default insurance, subprime mortgages, and hedge funds. For several years, advertising directed to the elderly and the financially strapped tempted homeowners with the lure of reverse mortgages: "Your home can be your ATM! Get money from it, finance that Bermuda vacation you have always wanted!" It was a patent contradiction to the advice that my generation grew up on: Own a home to own your future and to pass wealth on to your children. Instead, we were being told to "raid your savings!" Put John Wesley into to the trash bins of antiquated rules. Don't worry about protecting a possible inheritance for your children. No room for distributive justice in this advice. Nor was there any room in the jokes that Enron executives made about the high utility expenses they planned for "California grandmothers."

More than one mega-wealthy American has expressed mystification at the sudden economic losses that have cascaded around the human community under the name of a recession. Even the economists are scrambling to explain it all. For me and many of my world neighbors, we start explaining it in simple moral terms, opening ourselves to the contempt of those financial experts who are expert, most of all, in making huge salaries, bonuses, and stock gains for themselves. You can sell a mortgage to credit-unworthy customers if you hide from them the "balloon payment" in their future, along with escalating interest rates, and if you urge them to lie about their incomes. You offer credit card customers a line of credit without calling their attention to hard-to-read small print that informs them of how the interest rises to 29.5 percent after a certain period of default on payment. You keep undercover the company's hope that customers will never pay all of their monthly bill on time, so that they are forever paying high interest on their loan, just as the textile workers of yore forever owed the company store for their high-priced groceries. You can convince pension fund managers that bundles of mortgages are good investments because they spread the risks of defaults literally around the world. You can thereby hide the fact that no longer is anyone in particular *accountable* for dealing with the original buyers or sellers of those mortgages. Gone in this system is that old bank of my childhood, behind whose granite Roman columns worked staff who recognized you when you walked into those big quiet offices. Gone, too, any power in law or custom to aid your family once a staff in a faraway office forecloses on your mortgaged home, confronting you for the first time ever with the thought that your family may need to become street people.

Well, say the ideologues, that's the way the system works. You who invest in it should know about risk, the uncertain benefits of buying mortgages, bonds, or stock. Nature sometimes puts us all at risk with its hurricanes, floods, and diseases. So does the economic system. New competition is always a threat. Why shouldn't foreigners also be free to believe that "greed is good," including the greed that benefits oneself at the expense of others? Perhaps it is wise, along this ideological road to prosperity, to post signs and barriers—not in small print— that warn travelers to beware of thieves and other agents of greed. That is: Beware of an Ayn Rand who proudly signs the sky of her universe with "$," who contemptuously dismisses charity, government subsidies for the poor, objections to mega-million executive salaries and objections to corporate "restructuring" that eliminate thousands of jobs while increasing the bonuses of the officers who eliminate them.

Shot through all this ethical system is deafness to even a whisper of distributive justice. That version of justice some Americans associate exclusively with communism, which calls for just distribution of the wealth generated by the collective efforts of individuals, corporations, and governments. Executives like Jeff Skilling dismiss as "air headed" any limit on executive or investor incomes. But in doing so, they also dismiss from their awareness or worry the cost of mega-salaries and bonuses to the middle and low wage-earners of their organizations. Executives offered rewards for firing 10 percent of their workers should reject that version of reward out of hand. A profit, a salary, a compensation of any kind gained at the expense of imposing huge damages on individuals, families, and the common good are unjust by definition, once the definition of "justice" includes questions of the fair distribution of gains and just rewards for those who may have had major roles in achieving the gain but who also have power to grab most of the gains for themselves.

Not long ago, before he died, the business guru Peter Drucker recommended a ratio of approximately 1:25 for the distribution of salary levels in corporations. Between 2006 and 2008, even as they were being propped up by billions of government money, the biggest twenty American banks paid out $3.2 billion in bonuses to their one hundred highest-ranking executives, an average of $32 million per banker. In 2008, those same banks laid off 160,000 employees.[7] Rare indeed was any public expression of chagrin from the executive suites or any bow to notions of justice. In 1980, the low-to-highest salary ratio across the spectrum of the largest American corporations was 1:40. By year 2000, the ratio was 1:345, which meant that all lids were off. Notions of distributive justice are one of the lids. Law and discretion are among the others. On the discretionary side, I admire greatly those corporations that deny bonuses to executives in times of layoffs, that reduce high salaries for the sake of saving jobs, and that adopt policies for the distribution of profits whereby all in the firm gain some when times are good and all suffer some when times are bad.

Far from simple-mindedness, this reversion to distributive justice ought to be one of the measures of a revival of integrity among religious believers worldwide. The journalist Tom Oliphant once asked the late Ted Kennedy "Where does [your] rabid concern about poverty come from?" The senator "looked at me like I was from Mars. And he said, 'Have you never read the New Testament?'"[8] It was a reply as right as it was unconventional, right at least for people who want to be considered Christians. In the current struggles of ordinary people to understand and survive the Great Recession, I wish that more members of churches would dare to think and speak about things economic from Kennedy's biblical *perspective*. The prophet Amos knew little about mortgages, but he knew how the poor could be further impoverished for debt collection on as little as the cost of "a pair of shoes" (Amos 2:6). Jesus of Nazareth had nothing to say about credit default insurance or corporate bonuses, but he had a lot to say about the folly of wealth-worship. Modern capitalistic systems enable some adventurous investors to make a lot of money. That they sometimes make it at the expense of others cannot be denied. But a Bible-tutored conscience does not celebrate financial success achieved at the expense of damage to the poor. Nor can it celebrate competition between CEOs for the prestige of who is paid the highest. If wealth can be a worthy end of human effort, that end is not aggrandizement of power and prestige but an increased power to serve the needs of known and unknown neighbors. The chief end of a surplus ought to be to help neighbors who barely scrape by.

The mega-wealthy who turn large portions of their wealth into foundations for public service deserve our admiration. From Andrew Carnegie and John D. Rockefeller, Jr. to Bill Gates and Warren Buffett, we have examples of Americans who know that the chief end of human life is not wealth but service. I said once to the board of a foundation that my only envy of the wealthy is for their privilege of giving money away, a view based on the empirical truth of the New Testament, "It is more blessed to give than to receive" (Acts 20:35). I said this with full awareness that by world standards most Americans are relatively wealthy. The old advice "give all you can" applies to us all. To our shame in America, on average our poor give away a larger percentage of their incomes than does our middle class.

For their convictions about distributive justice, Christians in this society have to be willing to endure the scorn of others who steer their lives by a contrary ethic. The practice of this ethic will produce collisions with the engines of greed and the lures of truth-shading in ordinary economic transactions. In none of this, will an ethic based on religion leave the "religious" with the right to claim innocence in the roles they assume in modern economies. Ethical fundamentals will be a trustworthy start on some hazardous journeys. They will protect travelers from starting on a pilgrim's progress toward prosperity on a road that begins with the overhead sign: "Forget the dangers of greed."

For the retired of my generation, no issue of distributive justice cuts deeper into our self-interest than the question of how our government should serve not only our welfare but the welfare of the children and grandchildren of coming generations. In the early twenty-first century, the American elderly live in the richest society in history. In spite of recession, we have more wealth to pass on to our heirs than any other generation in history. We have much reason to ask about just and unjust distribution of this wealth to our scarcely-living world neighbors. But an easily forgotten dimension of distributive justice concerns intergenerational time: our obligations to those children and grandchildren. Some of them already doubt that they will ever, on average, be as rich as their parents and grandparents. In particular, they doubt that either Social Security or Medicare will be available for them. In 2009, those prospects look very dim indeed as they see us elders scrambling to protect the diminishing worth of our savings. One has to sympathize with those retirees in Florida described by a journalist in 2008 as "in grief. Their money died."

But not all of our retiree money has died. How do we conserve what is left? How shall we deal with the good fortune that past governments awarded us in Social Security and Medicare? Retirees can be greedy, too. Justice distributed between our needs and that upcoming generations has not yet claimed the attention of many Americans over sixty-five. We need to ponder the effects of generous government benefits upon any duplication of that generosity in the lives of Americans not yet born. In several clear-headed books, billionaire Peter G. Peterson has arrayed the intimidating statistics. Peterson calls for a rigorous combination of financial reality, just taxation, and some of the moral discipline implied in the definition of a "blameless" person in Psalm 15:4: "one who swears to his own hurt and does not change, who does not put out his money at interest and does not take a bribe. . . ." So far, even Peterson has not figured out exactly how to fit concepts of distributive justice-over-time to the statistics. When economists and moralists do work out that fit, they will be calling on my generation to cut back on some of our privileges, our incomes, and our unwillingness to be taxed. We will have to engage in much reflection on how we can work to ensure that our investments not only pay off to ourselves but to future members of our personal and our global human family.

It will be difficult for most of us Jewish and Christian Americans to discover how Psalm 15 relates to our condition in the recession years after 2009. Its prohibition against taking interest on loans runs counter to modern economics and its engines of lending and investing. (From the Koran, Muslims have the same problem.) As things stand in our economy, our children are right to hope that they will someday inherit resources we might bequeath to them. But the hopes of coming generations provide no easy excuse for making the highest possible returns on investments that make Americans rich while keeping undereducated African children poor and our fellow citizens burdened with credit card debt. I want no part, not even for the benefit of my children, in a 30 percent return on credit card loans.

Again, all mixed in with these ruminations has to be some revival of the old idea a just price for money. As of the early 1980s, the U.S. Congress buried that idea when it abolished the federal law against "usury." If markets rule every price, who can conceive of what usury *is*? The old Hebrews saw it more simply: no interest-taking at all, at least from a neighbor of one's own tribe. Maybe interest from a stranger: maybe at a "just" price? But no transaction was acceptable that reduced strangers to poverty or confiscated the security which backed up a day's loan to them; for example, the coat which they needed at night to keep warm. Beginning to entertain the idea that borrowers should pay creditors something for the use of the money, Calvinists began to say "yes" to interest and profit, but they were super-cautious about the line between justice and exploitation. A recent document of the Presbyterian Church (USA), a descendant of Calvin, proposes that the absence of a concept of usury, and an ethical restraint on interest rates, is wrong in principle. Credit card companies, the document notes, prefer customers who never pay off their debt, for at an interest rate of 30 percent that debt is enormously profitable to the company. Furniture stores can make a lot of profit from poor customers unaware that buying on time can quadruple their final costs. Most of all, "predatory mortgage lending drains wealth from families, destroys the benefits of home ownership, and often leads to foreclosure."[9]

The critique of capitalistic ethics in Psalm 15 is radical. It requires the modern Jew and Christian to ask: might certain practices of debt-marketing, commissions for sales, mega-bonuses for mortgage bundlers, and abandonment of interpersonal responsibility for the fate of primary borrowers, add up benefits of capitalists gained at the expense of neighbors? Speak only enough truth to serve greed and reach for profits that bribe conscience into silence? Is it not time for Christian Americans to challenge the orthodoxies of capitalism with orthodoxies closer to the New Testament? Dare Christians warn against earning money when the costs include increased poverty, job loss, deception of borrowers, and a diminished common good? The language of both testaments is supposed to be the first language of the church. As that Presbyterian paper on usury concludes, "The very definition of what constitutes lives of true abundance is the native tongue of the church."

All of us, not only those who profess a religious faith and ethic, are audience for these irksome questions. As one personal case in point, I end with a postscript concerning an investment decision that has much troubled Peggy and Don Shriver "in the year of our Lord 2009."

Postscript: The Company You Keep

My mother resorted often to the old proverb, "You are known by the company you keep." Neither she nor I imagined that one could turn that adage in the direction of economic ethics by asking if "company" could also be "corporation." That turn preoccupied James Kuhn and me over many a class hour and manuscript page as we considered the ethical quality of a corporate stock investment worth calling "socially responsible." Among others in the SR movement, we tended toward measuring the responsibility of business companies against standards of fair labor practices, environmental protection, resistance to racism, and corporate contributions to the common good.

When implementing such standards for the management of our individual investment decisions, many of us depend on a broker committed to those standards. But occasionally, we do make an investment choice on our own. A personal case in point concerns a long-range investment of a mere $5,000 which we made thirty-five years ago in a local North Carolina bank.

We were about to leave the state after seventeen years of growing affection for its people. We wanted to leave behind some token of that, so we invested in stock of a newly organized bank headquartered in Winston-Salem. Some years later, the bank merged with another corporation. In the meantime, we left dividends in the account, and by year 2000. the stock was worth $300,000. It was our taste of capitalistic luck.

In the winter of 2009, we noted from the annual report of the company that in December its upper executives had declined to take their usual annual bonus. We wrote a letter to the president thanking the bank for that gesture in light of the crisis in the banking business worldwide. With a CEO salary of almost $1 million, his sacrifice was moderate to say the least.

Then in the summer of 2009, there came in the business section of *The New York Times* an account of the devotion of the bank board chairman to the books and the philosophy of Ayn Rand. Not only was it his habit to distribute copies of *Atlas Shrugged* to new employees of the bank. He had also endowed faculty chairs at Wake Forest University for the promotion of Rand's materialist, libertarian, and atheist philosophy of economic striving. As a longtime resident of the South, this news astonished me: not that some business leaders might affirm Rand's views of the human world, but that the head of a regionally-based corporation would so publicly endorse and promulgate those views in a local culture well known for its numerous Bible-believers. Might customers of this bank raise concerns for how its board chairman was using his wealth? For objection to his hard-fisted public contempt for certain basic Christian beliefs, would prudence alone suggest that a bank chairman keep quiet about his atheism and materialism?

The issue for the Christian investor is difficult indeed. In this country, we believe in freedom of speech and belief. Most Americans are not shocked if a Buddhist is elected head of, say, the humane society or a Muslim becomes a leading government economist. At the very least a southern-born Presbyterian might well wonder if a fan of Ayn Rand sitting at the head of a major bank is good for the bank's image in a market crowded with Christians of all stripes. How many of them care about how a board chair uses his million-dollar salary? Are they more than willing to segregate his philosophy from the profitability of his company? So far we this philosophy has not pushed company policy to deny charitable donations to various causes in its community, a denial that Ayn Rand would certainly commend. To be sure, it would be a very southern gesture for a corporation to distribute copies of the Bible to its new employees, though it would be a test of its devotion to religious liberty if some of those employees asked for the Koran instead. Should new employees be given a choice—Bible, Koran, or *Atlas Shrugged*?

The issue for this stock holder is whether the outside activity of a business leader should prompt (1) protest to management, (2) selling one's stock and investing it in a company whose leaders are more to one's ethical liking, (3) keeping the stock as modest leverage for continuing the protest, or (4) giving the stock away at once to not-for-profit charity. In reflection on my own past in the South, I have wondered if a local CEO had personally endowed academic chairs for the promotion of the views of the Ku Klux Klan, would I have been justified in divesting from that company? Many of us supported the boycott of investment in South African companies during the apartheid era, even when the companies had only a remote role in sustaining that racist system. One assumes that a large majority of Americans would probably protest the election of a professing communist to the head of a major corporation. If so, how is the issue different from a CEO whose makes no secret of his admiration of two pillars of the communism which Ayn Rand fled, namely its materialism and its atheism?

Close to the heart of ethical honesty here is the reality of the compromises which all ethically-minded people accept when, knowingly or unknowingly, they lend money to businesses that serve causes that are not in conformity with one's deepest beliefs. The Social Responsibility in Investment movement finds favor with many liberally minded people for its avoidance of association with firms that damage the environment, practice covert racism or sexism, produce weapons for an unjust war, or hide their profits from tax collectors. If firms so managed are to be avoided for investment on ethical grounds, why not avoidances on grounds of basic religious belief? Naturally the first ethical option might be divestment, but that option does not exactly clear the conscience. What a shame, I reflect, that I have these years kept company with a bank whose founder and leader espouses views of the world so profoundly antagonistic to my own and so dangerous, I believe, to the health of a human society.

I know: there are no innocent associations in the worlds of economics and politics, not to mention religion! Perhaps the first sin humans need to acknowledge is our affection for claiming innocence. In the face of some ethical dilemmas, there are no conscience-clearing solutions. Yet, for lack of absolute goods, many a chance of relative good can get ignored. My teacher, H. Richard Niebuhr, said it best: "If we can do nothing perfectly, we can do some things imperfectly as alternative to doing nothing at all."

As this is written, the Shrivers are in the process of selling all of their stock in this bank, committing it to charitable causes. It's our contradiction of Randian principles. It's also a touch of irony and a sliver of belated investor repentance.

NOTES

1 Niall Ferguson, *The Ascent of Money: A Financial History of the World* (New York: The Penguin Press, 2008), 29–30.

2 By then, the COL index was close to seven, that is, my income in 2009 dollars was $42,000.

3 Ferguson, *The Ascent of Money*, 159.

4 Dwight Garner, *New York Times*, 18 September 2009, C29, quoting from from Robert Skilelsky's biography of John Maynard Keynes. "Keynes ultimately saw economics not as a natural science but a moral one. He was loath to rely on pure mathematics and risk models. Not everything could be reduced to numbers."

5 Ferguson, *The Ascent of Money*, 171.

6 Careful students of the early Karl Marx will point out that he had a form of respect for human personhood and the hope for a utopian future that embraced non-material promises. But that is a matter for the historians to parcel out. It was to common experience that Jesus appealed when he observed that "humans do not live by bread alone."

7 "Tackling the Titans," *The Nation*, September 28, 2009, 3.

8 Tom Oliphant, quoted in PBS *NewsHour*, August 26, 2009, *The Christian Century*, September 28, 2009, 9.

9 Office of the General Assembly of the Presbyterian Church, *A Reformed Understanding of Usury for the Twenty-First Century*, approved by the 2006 General Assembly (Louisville: Office of the General Assembly, 2006), 11–13.

Chapter 10

A LETTER TO OUR GREAT-GRANDCHILDREN: ON FAITH, HOPE, AND LOVE

❧

In recent years, the phrase "full disclosure" has come into fashion within the United States. It serves to warn people that "what I have to say" can have some hidden background that might compromise the honesty of the writer or speaker, as writing about parenthood when one has never been a parent. My full disclosure for this letter is simply to say that I have plenty of reasons to want to communicate with my great-grandchildren, but I am fully aware that I am writing to folk whom I will probably never see and who will never see me. I am far from confident that anything I write here in the year 2009 will ever be read by anybody living in, say, the year 2060. That is the year when, I imagine, you will have reached adulthood as the children of my four Iowa grandchildren. They are likely to become your parents in years 2030–2040. As your great-grandfather, born in 1927, I do not expect to be alive on earth in those years. If you know who I was, you probably also know about your great-grandmother Peggy.

To our love and marriage your grandfather Timothy owes his existence.

So, you might say, this is a strange, useless message addressed from a person you cannot have known to persons I cannot ever know. But a very human urge prompts this letter: *hope.* A scientist named Loren Eiseley said that humans are the only creatures capable of passing messages back through the doors of their own tombs. People of one human generation have no right, nor sufficient wisdom, for telling future generations just what to think or how to live. But we have every right and duty to record our hopes for them.

So, I hope for you:

That you are alive, and well.

It may seem strange that anyone should find hopeful the mere fact that you exist in the year 2060. To our chagrin, my generation of humans has reason to wonder if future generations will survive us, for we have inserted into the history of this planet two dreaded dangers to the future of our species: war on a mass scale and ecological damage. My century, the one we number the twentieth, destroyed at least 175,000,000 humans in wars. The war into which I was drafted as a soldier came to its awful end in explosions over two Japanese cities that killed 200,000 people. It is quite possible that, had World War II not ended then, I would have been a soldier in the American invasion of Japan, scheduled to begin two months before my eighteenth birthday. Eighteen-year-olds were a vulnerable age group, worldwide, in 1945.

Even more vulnerable were the men, women, and children who became the chief casualties of that and every other war of my twentieth century. Scientists contemporary with me have the dubious honor of having invented weapons that could kill the entire human population of earth and many other species. We humans have had a hard time surviving the "thousand natural shocks that flesh and blood are heir to"—disease, accident, tornadoes, floods, and earthquakes. The depressing fact of my time has been that we have added a unique danger: our own weapons could finish us off on all seven continents.

We now know that the whole earth and all of its species are vulnerable to the damages that humans have inflicted on our biosphere. We have been ecologically careless and foolishly arrogant. We have built our industrial civilization at the expense of our global cloaks of air, water, and soil. In my twentieth-century years, millions of us woke up to these facts. Our wars against nature and each other compel us to hope for you a worldwide retreat from these two forms of human violence. Our lives and that of all life on earth depend upon that retreat.

But I write this letter in the confidence that you now exist! If you do, that's defense enough against our dread that the worst in *Homo sapiens* will soon defeat the best. So it is no superficial hope in me that envisions you alive in the year 2060. Alive, and well, too, I hope. The medical scientists of my time were good soldiers in the "war" against the diseases which have brought early death to countless generations of us humans. You are their beneficiaries. In 1910, a Harvard philosopher named William James encouraged readers to consider "The Moral Equivalent of War." Medical combat against disease qualifies as that equivalent. I don't like calling our efforts to sustain life by a word, "war," whose meaning is opposite that of "life." But "alive and well" is no small hope for anyone's future. You are healthier and longer-of- life, I hope, than any other cohort of humans in 50,000 years of our history.

That brings to my mind a second hope for you:

That you are daily grateful for your life and all that has made your life possible

As your grandfather Timothy may have mentioned to you, his brother Gregory and he (with some helpers) built a country home for Peggy and me in the Berkshire hills of eastern New York State. A few items in that house Timothy may have chosen to keep. I have a hunch that he will have picked out two photographs on our walls as part of his inheritance. One is a photo that was taken on November 19, 1863, soon after the invention of photography. The other is from the 1880s. It is a portrait of my own great-grandfather, surrounded by his wife and nine children. One of the children, who at the time was about twenty years old, is the young woman who would become the mother of my father in 1901. She was to die in 1938 when I was ten years old. Hers was the first death to make that event real to me.

Like Alfred, her husband-to-be, she was born in the year following that other photo: 1864. Your lives and mine were deeply influenced by both of those years. The 1863 photo pictures a crowd around a platform erected on a momentous battlefield: Gettysburg. It shows a president of the United States, Abraham Lincoln, who has just finished uttering the 272 words of an address saying what he thought the war was about: ". . . that government of the people, by the people, and for the people might not perish from the earth."

On Second Thought

So there you are in 2060, biologically indebted to fathers and mothers whom you have never met and politically indebted to soldiers who fought to preserve the country where, I assume, you are living. Were I alive in the time of your own great-grandchildren in the twenty-second century, I would want to know if such a government had survived. Wars are colossal combinations of much evil and some good. The American Civil War preserved the union of the states; but more, it led to the abolition of slavery, one of the great negative blots on the history of this country. It took the death of some 620,000 Americans to get rid of that institution. Then it took us about a hundred more years to make sure that the descendants of the slaves would be counted as full citizens of this country. In my lifetime, the laws, the public protests, and the political movements that finally achieved this were good examples of James's "moral equivalent of war." I hope that, in some moments of your life, you experience gratitude that there is such a country as the United States for you to live in, and that the country is still worth your gratitude.

If you know about that Civil War, you know that it was not a perfect country then, and you know that it is not a perfect country in 2060. Slavery was a true curse on the early history of the United States. The racism in that curse lingers in my own time. I suspect it still lingers in yours. As a boy raised in the 1930s in Virginia, it took me quite a few years to understand what "racism" is and its deep contradiction to the words of that Gettysburg Address. I came to see that it was even more a contradiction to the Bible that my mother gave me at age fourteen. Of course, you may be living in a country better than the one I lived in. You may find it difficult to believe that once Americans called "black" were forbidden to live next door to Americans called "white," to eat in the same restaurants, to vote, to get jobs appropriate to their abilities and even to join the same church. Hopefully the struggles against these versions of inequality among citizens are so successful in your time that you think of all this as ancient history. If you do, you ought to be grateful for those ancestors of yours who helped deliver you from the effects of some of their sins. Is the United States of your time still existing? I hope so. Does it still have the scars and the diseases of injustice and assorted wrongs of neighbors against neighbors? I suspect so. In your time is this country still struggling with injustices to immigrants, Native Americans, Muslims, and poor people worldwide? I bet it is.

That you are happier to be human than to be merely American.

In my time, one of the great new facts about our species went under the name "globalization." The word implied that for the first time in our history we were bound together economically, politically, electronically, transportationally, and militarily. By 2060, folk of your time will find it strange that folk of mine would experience a bit of awe when they picked up a phone to call someone in Bangalore or pressed a few buttons to write an email to a friend in South Africa who replies five minutes later. With such instant communication, physical distances between earth's continents seemed to collapse. The problem was that other, different kinds of distance between human beings did not collapse. In the American election of 1940, a Republican candidate, Wendel Wilkie, took a plane trip around the world. When he returned, he held up a finger and said, "One world!" Some people made fun of Wilkie on that point. Much of the human world in that year was at war, and soon the United States would become part of that war. We were one, all right, one in our hostility to each other as well as in our growing interconnections.

My contemporaries often forgot that the idea of "humanity" is very old and that it takes more than technology to make us real neighbors to each other worldwide. In the year 2009, an economic recession happened so quickly across the world that even our smartest economists could not understand it. As I write, some two billion of my world neighbors (out of six billion) have been living on $2 or less a day. The recession compelled many to live, if at all, on less than $2. Many, as I write, are dying from cost of food, drugs, housing and sanitation that they cannot afford. How would you translate this statistic into your time? I hope you will find out. You will have lived in a better world if by 2060 the nations of earth have drastically reduced that terrible statistic.

It is a rather shaky hope, I confess. I have a deep, troubling respect for the power of human selfishness. When disaster threatens, we batten down our hatches, scramble for safety, and look first to protect ourselves, our immediate families, and our closest friends from the disaster. That's why, century after century, pessimists among us pelt the idea of "humanity" with rocks like, "Be practical. Look out for number one. Don't try to take on the world." Well, from my time into yours, the world has been taking on us. Martin Luther King, Jr. was being very practical when he said: "We must either live together as brothers and sisters or we will perish together as fools." When he said that, he drew from a certainty far older than twentieth century globalization. He spoke as a follower of Jesus, who called his disciples to "love one another" without distinction between one and another's race, geographic location, sex, age, wealth, obscurity, or fame. It took a long time for Christians to learn that, to act on their faith in Jesus, the Creator means to create "one new humanity" no longer divided by "walls of hostility"(Ephesians 2). In two thousand years, we have seen as much violation of that faith among Christians as fidelity. I do not blame anyone who sees in religion a force that builds as well as breaks down barriers. Humans are great wall-builders. Have you noticed that in your own time? God and God's believers have always needed a lot of help to break down the walls of hostility; the help of all world religions, for example, government laws, fair international trade, and political systems which require negotiation between the rich and the poor.

Okay, so the idea that the Chinese and the Nigerians are people as human as you are may be old stuff in your minds. If so, great! You are schooled by a lot more daily information about those neighbors than was possible in my own early years. I hope that, as an idea, "humanity" really is old stuff to you because you are meeting people every day from all the continents. On days when I ride the New York City subway, I often count the probable number of continents represented among the fifty people in a single subway car. But just being in the same set of seats does not guarantee real "neighborhood." We humans are on a long march towards real, affirming connection with each other. I am sure that the march will not be over in your lifetime. You too will have to struggle to meet the challenges of living in a planetary human home. And your temptation will be similar to mine: despair over our limited ability to "love our world neighbors as ourselves." You too will be tempted to settle for the philosophy recommended by Voltaire: "One must cultivate one's own garden." That motto is isolationist. It invites us to reduce our neighborly concerns to folk of our locality.

In sum, are any of us capable of responding to the needy cries of so many among those six billion, who in your time may be eight or ten? For centuries the *idea* of humanity has been a weakling in contests between the powers of race, nationality, wealth, weaponry, and prestige. You are probably as vulnerable as were we to political leaders who cry, "America first!" Only in my father's time, by the way, did this country really begin to reckon in its policies with the fact that isolation between regions of the earth is ultimately impractical. The "seventy-five year war" of 1914–1989 was the first real world war, and in many tragic ways that war still goes on as I write. Has it ended in your time? I hope so, but I do have my doubts. I know how the "me first" feeling in most of us humans is dangerous to neighborliness local and worldwide. This country of ours became mega-wealthy in my lifetime. We made some progress in believing that some of our wealth should be shared with the poor people of earth. But you will recognize how minuscule was our "progress" when I note that in 2007 the United Nations asked rich nations to devote seven-tenths of one per cent of their annual national economic product (seven cents out of every one hundred dollars) to the alleviation of poverty worldwide. A stingy goal! But it would be progress of a sort. The United States government in 2009 was offering a scant 2 cents instead of 7 to this cause, though with the voluntary gifts of Americans in churches and other world-conscious organizations, we may come close to that 7 cents.

I guess that, in my hope for your personal future and your connections to your family, a church, a political movement, or any other window of your life onto the lives of your neighbors worldwide, you are affirming those neighbors in the ways you spend your money, talk with your family, write your political leaders, select stories to read from the internet, speak up in a church, and plan your travels. The discipline of paying regular attention to strangers around the globe is rigorous. Not everybody around you will be shouting "hurrah!" when you tell them that you try to practice the ancient Jewish-Christian rule of giving 10 percent of your annual income to the needs of others. I know people poor and rich who give more than that. They set an embarrassing example to governments that are always under the pressures of insular interests. I hope that your spirit and your life habits constantly hold at bay the threats of insularity. You can't be a real member of a human family by looking out only for the family in your own house.

But to do justice to what I mean by that "family" business, here is another hope implied in all that I have written so far. It's very personal.

That you will fall deeply in love and will stay in that love permanently.

That photo of my great-grandfather and his family comes from a time when the love of man and woman was expected by most folk to result in a marriage that would last the lifetimes of the partners. In my lifetime, we westerners have experienced a so-called "sexual revolution" which began to sit very loose to that expectation. Divorce rates soared, and for people young and old the idea of lifelong marriage between two faithful partners began to seem an impossible ideal, especially when the young looked on the failed marriages of their own parents. Beyond the rising divorce rates, a greater diversity of views on marriage was reflected in unprecedented increases in homosexual partnerships and single-parent families. For many, it was as if there must be no standards for shaping one's sexuality, beyond just "what feels good." And, thanks to new technologies of birth control, the complication of unwanted babies seemed eminently avoidable.

In all of these changes, the idea of marriage as a lifelong union of two people—bound together sexually, domestically, and parentally—developed a reputation for being absurd. Few people of all ages doubted that sexual experience is one of life's great pleasures. For sure: it feels good! I have the notion that nature means sex to feel so good that the perpetuation of our species is almost guaranteed. But why connect it exclusively to the relation of two persons "till death do us part"? Why treat it as somehow at its best in the constrictions of marriage? Why even connect it with parenthood? And why fence it in with laws that require married couples to take care of each other "in sickness and in health, in plenty and in want, in joy and in sorrow, as long as we both shall live"?

It may be hard for you to believe, but the lives of my two parents and my five pairs of uncles and aunts underwent not a single divorce. Whether all twelve of these elders were supremely happy in their marriages, I did not know. I did know that divorce was always a possible end of a marriage, but my immediate family somehow shunned that possibility. In my own later years, I came to realize that divorce was a more humane decision for some couples than their determination to "stick it out on behalf of the children." I knew how bereft some of my own friends felt when one of their parents died. But seldom did I encounter marriages in which the love had obviously died, nor did I get close personally to the grief that one divorcing partner often leaves behind in the life of the other.

Okay, you can read this as how ancient is the history in this letter. I encourage you to become *really* ancient in your perspectives on this great matter. Over time, humans have found in marriage a humanizing power that is very, very special. Sadly enough, the "sexual revolution" of my time has prompted some young people, in an honest moment, to ask: "What's so special about it?" From my own life as a married man of fifty-six years (as of 2009 and counting!), I have one deep answer to that poignant question: the special something is a love that can neither be reduced to sex nor separated from it.

Not long ago, I served on a panel in Northern Ireland to discuss the desire of two young women to become legally married. I was asked to reflect on the ethics of such a relationship. To the surprise of some, I turned to the first three chapters of Genesis which recounts, in mythological form, the creation of the world. There, the Creator makes a human in the very image of the divine. But the creature is incomplete. "It is not good for the man to be alone." So a companion, woman, comes into being. And so, a later verse explains, "a man leaves his father and his mother and cleaves to his wife, and they become one flesh." Here, companionship and fidelity are the marks of real marriage. In my time, gay and lesbian partners could convincingly claim that, by those standards, they were married. However controversial, this "take" on marriage from Genesis is a refusal to place reproduction of the species as the only true end of a sexual relation.

Lots of anthropologists observe that the idea of a "companionate" marriage is young in history. I'm not so sure. There are many examples of the joy of loving, sexual companionship in the Bible itself. See for example the love story of Isaac and Rebekah in Genesis 24, which ends with the touching words, "Isaac . . . took Rebekah, and she became his wife; and he loved her. So Isaac was comforted after his mother's death."

To companionship, much in the Bible wants to add the benefits of sexual fidelity. In my time, lots of folk have thought to themselves and each other: "What's so bad about multiple sexual partners, even if you are legally married?" The business of "legally" worries them. Law in old times and new has often taken marriage as an affirmation of ongoing obligation of a man and a woman to care for each other come what may. The whole idea of adultery depends on the validity and the humane promise of such obligation. It is certainly possible that two modern people might enter an "open" marriage covenant with the understanding that each will allow the other to have other liaisons if they so wish. But that implies a very superficial notion of covenant and promise. Such an agreement usually turns out lopsided, often in service to the freedom of men rather than women.

Out of half a century of being married, I have to testify that a really firm, fulfilling marriage makes the idea of turning to adultery the height of absurdity. Leave this deep well of joy in bed with this man and this woman for an occasional sip of somebody else? You must be kidding! Certainly marriage can decline into mere sips, leaving one or both partners thirsty for something better. Even a failed marriage, however, seems to leave residues of a surmise that another, more fulfilling relationship is worth hankering for. Most divorced people seek a new marriage, a tribute to something wonderful glimpsed even in the failure of the previous one. Cartoons about shaky love between two persons about to be formally married may have one or both partners muttering under their breaths, ". . . till death does us part or until someone more interesting comes along." People who consciously hedge their bets in this way are not ready to get married.

What I want most to testify to you here has little to do with law, society's expectations, or ideas of sexual freedom. I want to testify to a fact about my own life: the joy of my marriage to Peggy Ann Leu of Pella, Iowa, on August 9, 1953, and during all subsequent years down to right now. This marriage has been the principal joy of my life. Nothing in the successes of my professional career (I have had a few) compares with companionship. I have often felt shy about making this testimony, for I am super-conscious that not all marriages succeed, that divorce leaves much pain in its wake, that divorce is the better alternative to a vanished love, and that it is inconsiderate of the experience of other people to set oneself up as a model of happiness to which they should aspire. From respect for these cautions, the happiness in many marriages has often gone unspoken to others by both partners. But fact is: words cannot supply adequate testimony to many of the great joys of life, and this is one of them. For me, it was the best of them. Some of us, who are neither poets nor musicians, have to depend on smiles, laughter, and fifty years of mutual love to express what words alone cannot say. But words like these come easily to me: marriage for me has been the single greatest joy of my life.

To be sure, marriage begins in feelings for another, in physical urges which we often reduce to the word "sex." We use the word too abstractly. Sex is a magnet that attracts and enriches many another feature of a fulfilling partnership. It's like the flavor of a richly spiced Indian curry. You won't like it without the curry powder, but you enjoy curry powder as a special ingredient that pervades the whole dish.

I have referred in another essay to a Catholic friend who began her marriage in the usual Roman Catholic assurance that God mandated marriage chiefly for human reproduction, for babies. "But I have changed my mind on that," she said. "I now believe that the chief activity of marriage is conversation." Peggy and Don Shriver would vouch for that. That "one flesh" image encapsulates a lot of human experience. Regular sexual intercourse, certainly; but what about the hours in between? And the conversation that on occasion activates the intercourse? Add to that: days and days of "ordinary" details of living, all of which become occasions of joy because so abundantly shared, talked about, probed, and deepened.

Brother Lawrence, a Christian monk of great integrity, once wrote, "I can pick up a straw for the love of God." I hope that God is not displeased when I offer from my own years of marriage the testimony: "I can pick up a lot of straws from our dirty floor for love of Peggy. She picks up a lot for me. And somehow it's a pleasure."

Some years ago, when we had built our vacation home on a thinly populated hillside, a friend wanted to know: "What on earth do you two have to talk about all the months you stay there?" The answer is: everything on earth! Antoine Saint-Exupery once remarked, "Love is not just looking at each other but looking outward in the same direction." I'd vary that by saying: There are many electric "third rails" in great marriages, sources of power in causes to serve, pains to share, and world news to keep alert to. Such exterior events enrich and direct many an interior. In America of the 1980s, both partners were likely to undertake professional jobs outside the home. I am sure that one test of a growing marriage is the daily report which each partner brings home. Not to be interested in a partner's work outside the home is to be not really interested in her or him. W.H. Auden ended his great "Christmas Oratorio" with the hope that things outside a relation of genuine love would participate in its ongoing inside reality: that "at your marriage all its occasions shall dance for joy."

"One flesh" means all of this and more. Have I mentioned children? No, and the fact that I delay to mention them is important. The gift of children is the greatest "third" in that one-flesh relationship. They are the second momentous gift of a real marriage. They are the messages we count on transmitting to a future that we hope will outlast us.

So long as they live, parents never stop being parents. Even after they leave their first home, sons and daughters continue to tug at parental hearts. Real parenthood should last forever. If not, if parental loyalties dissolve, children suffer. If parents are already faithful companions of each other, their children have a safety net to depend on when times get tough for them. In strict analogy to their own marriage covenant, parents implicitly oblige themselves to children, too, when they pledge fidelity "in sickness and in health, in joy and in sorrow . . . so long as we both shall live." Happy the family sustained by strong sinews of that covenant! Parental love of children can survive divorce and death of one parent, but the strength of a two-parent, faithful partnership is an enormous benefit to children themselves. Research tends to demonstrate that.

A word about the "sorrow": there are no marriages that do not eventually experience it, and the experience can result in bonds stronger yet. The trauma of our struggle with the 1969 life of our older son, detailed in chapter 6 of this little book, had much sorrow in it, as does every illness and other crisis in the life of any family member. But aside from crises of life and love in one's nuclear family, the sorrows of neighbors worldwide bid for our constant attention, and one might even say that joy and sorrow inside one's home equips its members with an ability to empathize with joy and sorrow outside. The theologian Emil Brunner once alluded to "the problem of happy marriages." He probably meant the problem of a nuclear family willing to make itself an island of joy amid an ocean of misery. A problem, indeed. In 2009, one had to be news-numb not to think daily of widows and orphans left in the wake of wars, rampaging famine in African villages, and illnesses untreated in poor neighborhoods of the rich United States. It is easy to dismiss these suffering folk from one's mind in America, or to pretend that the loss of a beloved spouse or child in an African village hurts Africans less than it would hurt oneself. Suffering is probably the experience that brings us humans closest to each other. We can all identify with the realities of pain. Sadly, not all of us know what happiness is or how to appreciate it. It is hard in the midst of one's own suffering to celebrate the joys of others.

No two marriages are exactly alike in either their joys or their sorrows. I hope that you are in or soon will be in a terrific marriage. I can even hope that your experience of marriage will be crammed full of joys that exceed my own. I can hardly imagine that! I do not, however, expect any of my children or grandchildren to duplicate the mutuality of their forbears' marriages. Let the new-timers improve on the old-timers if possible! Meantime, I beg you: forgive these two great-grandparents, Peggy and Don Shriver, for wanting to testify to the glorious, rich, pervasive, permanent, and daily joy of their own marriage.

At our fiftieth anniversary party in 2003, I said to our friends there: "Some folk here have congratulated us on the 'achievement' of these fifty years. We thank you for that. But it has not been an achievement. It has been a gift." It has been so inscrutably a "given" that it never occurs to me to take credit for the love of Peggy Ann Leu Shriver for Donald W. Shriver, Jr. One might as well take credit for the rising of the sun, the mistake that Aesop's rooster made when he assumed that the sun rose because he crowed.

A great German theologian once wrote that religious faith first stirs in us humans from a dawning "sense of absolute dependence." A great marriage introduces deep dependence into the lives of two partners, but that dependence cannot be absolute, for death eventually deprives us all of each other. Is there anything in the world absolutely dependable? In particular, is there any love so durable that you can count on it to endure? It's a theological question. It concerns my final hope for you.

That you will always know that you are greatly loved.

In my lifetime, a "save the earth" movement gathered momentum, convincing many humans that, if we kept polluting the earth with our industrial and other waste, the planet would soon be uninhabitable. Science issued this warning, and many of us became sure that, if your generation of humans was to live happily, ours had to change our ways.

"Futuristic" films made vivid this warning and one of them in 2009, *The Age of Stupid*, pictured earth in the year 2055, that is, in your time. One reviewer summarized the theme of the film as scolding the human race "for having committed suicide." The title of the film refers to 2009, not 2055. Perhaps an alternate title could have been, "The Age of Me and Mine," an allusion to refusal of people in my time even to think about people in yours. The film, said the reviewer, might be food for pessimism about your future and our willingness to concern ourselves about it.

> "[It] may convince viewers that, practically speaking, it is already too late to act. Cynics may assume that the ethic of consumerism is too deeply instilled in us to be changed, as is the faith in capitalism, which depends on continuous growth. If so, we might as well put the coming horrors out of our minds and live for the moment, while hoping for a miracle."

Then the review ends with words that state the philosophic crisis that murmurs underneath this gloomy imagined futurism.

> A thread of needling gallows humor runs through *The Age of Stupid*. Near the end of the film [the chief character] wonders: "Why didn't we save ourselves? Was the answer that we weren't sure that we were worth saving?" He may have a point.[1]

I have spent most of my academic life in a field called Christian Ethics. The simplest assumption of the field might be stated: "I am worth saving. You are, too." Between the first and the second of those two sentences lie some vast contradictions, tragedies, struggles, and hope for this human race. Stay only with the first, and you have the view: "Me and mine first, let others take care of themselves."

We now know that this philosophy doesn't work even for the egocentric who adopts it. On a colossal scale, taking care of this one earth is a task that now belongs to this our one humanity. A relatively new difficulty in this task has to do with time-scale. The Iroquois Indian nation who once lived in New York State had a principle for thinking about their own and future times: "Act now with a mind for the next seven generations." That has proven a tough rule for lots of Americans. We are not very conscious of seven past generations, and we hardly know how to think of seven future ones.

I have written this letter to three generations ahead of my own. Maybe you will by now have learned to contemplate five or six! Even that may be too short, for great changes in this earth environment have usually taken thousands of years. At least we all could begin to think in terms of hundreds of years.

That murmur of despair projected into 2055 by the filmmaker, however, is the danger I hope that you and your contemporaries will mightily resist. As the film suggests, suicide is a real possibility for both individual and collective humanity. As one listens personally or collectively to that murmur of despair, it is possible to hear another, more positive murmur: "Yes, you are worth saving, and you are worth loving." To hear that latter murmur is to repair to a depth of faith and hope basically religious. Nothing in science can prove to you that your birth and life to date issue from a "love divine, all loves excelling." I have sung that hymnal phrase in many a Sunday of churchgoing, but I have come to believe that divine love has been lavishly spread around in my life in forms of earthly love—physical, parental, social, and historical. All of them offer evidence of a Love that resides in the heart of all things.

The nineteenth century Danish Christian Søren Kierkekaard remarked, "The thought of suicide has saved many a life." Having powers of decision is a definition of freedom. If to date your life has been mostly pleasant, well financed, and associated with some humans who convincingly love you, the question of suicide may never have entered your mind. If so, your good fortune gives you resources for paying attention to the miserable, the poor, and the little-loved lives of humans around you and in the world. That we all should pay such attention to others, as I have said, is basic to ethics. But for reasons underneath this "should," for the confidence that love is an actual power on earth making possible our love, we need a love from God communicated through the love of other humans.

Almost every psychologist and sociologist acknowledges that an unloved child seldom learns to love or to expect love. Some years ago an inadvertent experiment took place in a hospital on a ward for newborn infants. The staff was short on nurses. The cry of babies on that ward got no answers. Soon the cries stopped. Thus were prepared little humans for a life in which cries for help are useless. A shriveled selfhood was in the making.

To note this is simply to say that "we love because someone first loves us." That is a slight paraphrase of a line in the New Testament which names the "someone" as God our Creator in whose mind and will we humans are worth creating, worth loving, and worth surrounding with loving fellow creatures.

My own life has been so fortunate that suicide has never much tempted me. I had a friend in the 1950s who did commit suicide, and so far as we know he did so because of his sense of rejection by society in light of his homosexuality. One of the great cultural-ethical improvements of later decades in America was the "coming out" of homosexual persons into the light of day as an affirmation that their humanity, too, was worth saving. Out of such tragedies as my friend's suicide, some of us learned that, for sustaining the certainty that God loves us, the assist of human love is absolutely essential. God did not create us to live alone, nor did divine love mean to dispense with incarnation in the flesh of humans. We do love because God first loved us, and we do love because fellow humans have loved us into babyhood, childhood, maturity, and death. It is all one love.

So, here at the end, mine for you is a double hope: that you know that you are loved, and that from having been loved you are already empowered to love. Nothing in this hope is superficial, sentimental, or neglectful of "the slings and arrows of outrageous fortune" that touch us all. Painful disease, uncaring families, careless teachers, murderers, exploiters, terrorists, and other enemies of faith, hope, and love will not have disappeared from your world. In and against it all, we humans have been destined not only to survive in spite of our sins but to survive because of our love. That is why, in my own 2009, I can pray that you will know, believe, and rejoice in a faith that makes us all worth loving and worth saving. May such faith and power be yours as was hoped for long ago in another letter of greater authority than this one.

"Beloved, let us love one another. . . . If we love one another, God abides in us and his love is perfected in us" (John 4:7, 12).

NOTE

1 Stephen Holden, "An Alarm from 2055," *The New York Times*, 17 July 2009, C8.